Tom Adams

A Biography

TOM ADAMS
A Biography

F.A. Hoyos

FaHoyos

88-07-09

MACMILLAN
CARIBBEAN

To
Lady Adams

Who has given more to Barbados than anyone
else – her husband, her son and herself

First published 1988

Published by *Macmillan Publishers Ltd*
London and Basingstoke
*Associated companies and representatives in Accra,
Auckland, Delhi, Dublin, Gaborone, Hamburg, Harare,
Hong Kong, Kuala Lumpur, Lagos, Manzini, Melbourne,
Mexico City, Nairobi, New York, Singapore, Tokyo*

Printed in Hong Kong

British Library Cataloguing in Publication Data
Hoyos, *Sir* Alexander
   Tom Adams: a biography.
   1. Adams, Tom   2. Prime ministers——
   Barbados——Biography
   I. Title
   972.98'1'0094   F2041

ISBN 0–333–46332–3

Contents

Acknowledgements   vi
List of Photographs   vii
Foreword   viii

One   Signs of the Times   1
Two   Oxford   11
Three   London   18
Four   Father and Son   25
Five   Into the Arena   33
Six   Member of Parliament   41
Seven   Leader of the Opposition   51
Eight   I Want to Make a Confession   66
Nine   Prime Minister   78
Ten   The Pragmatist   98
Eleven   Caribbean Man   107
Twelve   Vision and Reality   124
Thirteen   The Last Strenuous Years   132
Fourteen   Interim Assessment   145
Fifteen   The Verdict of the Elected
             Representatives   161
Sixteen   Death Shall Have No Dominion   177

Chronology   193
Index   195

Acknowledgements

The author and publishers wish to acknowledge, with thanks, the following photographic sources:
Willie Alleyne Associates; Associated Press; Maurice E. Giles; Tony Hinds, courtesy of the Advocate's Librarian; F.A. Hoyos; Clyde Jones; Felix Kerr; Graham Norton; Errol Nurse, Barbados Government Information Service; Popperfoto; the *Sun*; United Nations; White House, Washington.

The *cover photograph* is courtesy of Willie Alleyne Associates, Barbados.

The publishers have made every effort to trace the copyright holders, but if they have inadvertently overlooked any, they will be pleased to make the necessary arrangements at the first opportunity.

List of Photographs

1   With his mother, Grace.
2   Tom at 9, a pupil of Harrison College.
3   Tyrol Cot.
4   The Oxford graduate.
5   At the BBC.
6   In an East End Settlement, London, early 1950s.
7   With his fiancée.
8   Gray's Inn Chapel: a new bride and groom.
9   Tom, Genevieve and Douglas, 1964.
10 A family group at 'Sunset'.
11 With his father, Sir Grantley Adams, at the Bar.
12 Sworn in as Prime Minister.
13 With Genevieve, at the sixteenth anniversary celebrations of Nigeria.
14 At UN headquarters, Tom with Secretary-General Kurt Waldheim.
15 Ilaro Court.
16 With Genevieve and their son Rawdon at the World Trade Center, Manhattan.
17 With the Queen and Commonwealth heads, June 1977.
18 With Canadian Premier Pierre Trudeau at the Commonwealth Conference, June 1977.
19 A gathering at Tyrol Cot, May 1978.
20 Tom addressing the BLP Conference, 1978.
21 With President Carter in Washington, DC.
22 With Dr Eric Williams.
23 Gardening at his home in St George, 1979.
24 With President Kenneth Kaunda, August 1979.
25 Returning from Commonwealth Finance Ministers Conference in Malta.
26 Surrounded by Barbadian nationals during a meeting in London.
27 Election campaign, Bridgetown, Barbados, June 1981.
28 Taking the oath of allegiance for the second time.
29 With Mrs Margaret Thatcher.
30 With President Reagan and Nancy Reagan.
31 Going out to bat in Barbados.
32 On a tour of Speightstown with Lionel Craig, MP.
33 Canvassing.
34 On his way to deliver the 1982–3 Budget speech.
35 At the BLP Christmas party, 1983.
36 Reopening the clay preparation plant at Greenland, St Andrew, July 1983.
37 A Russian-made AK-47 from Grenada, November 1983.
38 Senior public officers from the Commonwealth.
39 With Police Commissioner Reid and Chief of Staff, Defence Force, Rudyard Lewis.   *Prescod*
40 A final salute.

Foreword

I hope that readers in Barbados and elsewhere will emphathise with me in the sensitive and complex task I have undertaken in writing the biography of Tom Adams so soon after his death. He was a national and West Indian leader who created waves in the quarter-century in which he flourished.

The special advantage I can claim is the close relationship I have long enjoyed with the Adams family — Grantley, Grace and Tom. Many years ago a sister of mine was married to a brother of Grantley's. I hope that all this will not be held against me. I was always closer to Grantley and Tom than to the gentle and unassuming Guy Adams who worked in the Civil Service all his life and never rose above the rank of Senior Clerk, owing to the nature of the times in which he functioned.

All of this may not save me from the charge that this biography of Tom is merely a work of family piety. That is a risk that I am prepared to take. Actually, my special relationship with the Adams family has enabled me to obtain information that would not otherwise have been available to me. Much of the documentation on which ultimate assessments will have to be made is not yet accessible.

The present work may be regarded as a first statement. If the vigour of my tender years is maintained for another decade I may be able to write a better biography of Tom, supported by more evidence and documentation. His meteoric rise to political power and prominence was not exceeded by the dramatic suddenness of his death.

My first attempt at a biography appeared in 1964 as *The Rise of West Indian Democracy*. This was cordially welcomed by a number of friends, particularly C.L.R. James, and I was encouraged to produce a better study of Sir Grantley some ten years later when more information became available. It was published as *Grantley Adams and the Social Revolution* (1974).

Before Tom's return to Barbados in 1963 he was a comparatively unknown quantity. That was soon to change. His election to office as party leader and Leader of the Opposition in 1971 was not a succession but the result of his proven ability and leadership skills.

I have tried to build the biography around a centralising theme. And what I hope will emerge from the text is Tom's political mission — his conscious attempt to extend his father's own mission, to improve the management of public sector organisation and of central government, to develop the society physically and culturally, to commit Barbados to participation in arrangements to guarantee regional security and to realise Sir Grantley's dream of a united and self-governing West Indies.

That is the agenda that was uniquely his and with his death it proved impossible to sustain the momentum.

I have to thank all those who read this book in manuscript and made suggestions, comments and criticisms — Henry Forde, Fred Gollop, Billie Miller, Louis Tull, Ezra Alleyne and those who prefer to remain anonymous in view of what they regard as the hazards of the present time.

I think I should make special mention of Sir Keith Hunte, the Pro-Vice Chancellor of the University of the West Indies and Principal of the Cave Hill Campus. Once my pupil, he is now my guide and mentor. I take the liberty of saying this because he has read most of my books in manuscript with scrupulous care and attention, making invaluable comments and criticisms. If this book does not measure up to his expectations, it is certainly no fault of his.

Special mention should also be made of George Griffith, my enthusiastic and unpaid research assistant, who indefatigably facilitated access to many records.

Above all, I must acknowledge the help and encouragement of my wife who typed and retyped countless pages to cope with the frequent changes and alterations that were made in the manuscript. Without her industry, patience and tolerance, this work would never have been finished.

ONE

Signs of the Times

1

The atmosphere at St Michael's Girls' School was charged with gloom and apprehension. For three anxious days, the staff and pupils had been waiting to hear what was the fate of the expectant mother and of the child who was taking a long time to arrive in this world.

They would never forget Tuesday, Wednesday and Thursday of that week in September. For it was only on the third day that their colleague and teacher had survived the dangers of surgery and the child was safely delivered. There were lusty cheers throughout the school, expressing relief and joy when the news of the happy event reached the children. Tom Adams was born on 24 September 1931. To the average reader this may read like melodrama, but it comes straight from the staid pages of Hansard.[1]

Grace Thorne had been appointed to the staff of St Michael's in 1928, the first year of the school's existence. She stayed for one year, leaving in 1929 when she was married to Grantley Adams. That event was the cause of much excitement in the school where it was regarded as high romance. But to the world beyond the confines of that little community it was a different matter.

Grace came from a privileged family. For the daughter of a prominent white merchant to marry a black man, handsome though he was and already distinguished in his profession, was a source of much grief and sore distress. Indeed, some months before her marriage, she deemed it expedient to leave her home and stay with her friends, the Hynams, at 'Woodside' in Bay Street. It was from there that she went to the Church in St John, where the wedding was performed by the Rector of the parish, the Rev. H.B. Gooding, an old friend of Grantley's from Oxford days.

Though she left St Michael's Girls' School at the time of her marriage, Grace kept in touch with the staff and pupils, visiting them frequently. She remained a close friend and that is why the long travail that produced her only child was followed with such anxiety by the teachers and girls there.

After her marriage, most of her friends remained loyal and this helped to maintain her calm and equable spirit. In spite of the pain of childbirth, she rejoiced when her son was born. But this was not to be the end of her anxiety, for the child was born a 'blue baby' and had to be dipped in hot and cold water to save it from the fate of still-birth.

The manner of his coming into the world did not save him from a formidable list of names. His father wanted him to be called John after the great British advocate, Sir John Simon. Grantley himself was honoured by the name Sir John by those who admired his prowess at the Bar. But, by a curious mischance, the name on his son's birth certificate was spelt 'Jon'.

His mother liked the name Michael and thought that Geoffrey wasn't bad either. Moreover, she wanted to show her gratitude to the doctor, Gerald Manning, who had brought her and her son out of the valley of the shadow of death and she therefore added Manningham to her son's name. But she liked the name Tom best of all. So her son started life with an impressive list of names — Jon Michael Geoffrey Manningham Tom Adams, though Tom was not added to the names with which he was christened.

2

During the early years of his life, Grace was concerned over the frailty of her son's health. He was afflicted, but more severely than others, with all the ailments which children endure, with the sole exception of rheumatic fever. She brought him along during that hazardous period, using all the resources of love and ingenuity. She played cricket with him on the beach and on the grounds of Tyrol Cot and allowed him to wander at will in the neighbourhood, where he made many friends.

So for the mother's sake the child was dear, and dearer was the mother for the child. The words of the poet explain the close and intimate comradeship that began between Grace and her son from the earliest years — an understanding that was to last until the end.

To the anxiety of nurturing her son during this time were soon added problems of a different nature. Her husband first entered the House of Assembly in 1934 and right from the outset he began to make noises such as had never before been heard in that patrician Chamber.

The effect of Grantley's outbursts in the House was perhaps predictable. He was regarded as a dangerous agitator and caused much discomfort among the oligarchs by reminding them of the distress in the country and warning them of the lessons to be learnt from the French Revolution. The solicitors of Bridgetown, who were almost exclusively white and closely associated with the ancien régime, began to withdraw their briefs from Grantley. The result was that his lucrative practice was soon reduced to a trickle and he had to rely mainly on such modest fees as the poor could afford to pay for his services. At least on one occasion, he had to be reminded by the Secretary of the Board of Education that his son's school fees at Harrison College were not paid at the appropriate time.[2]

In these circumstances, Grace was forced to go back to work in order to help meet the expenses of her household. In 1928 St Michael's Girls' School had welcomed her with open arms, for it was established as a learning centre for the poor and the disadvantaged; and they recognised in Grace qualities that were admirably suited to train the children who were placed in her care.

The situation was changed from the beginning of Grantley's stormy career in the House. The governing body, composed mostly of middle-class Conservatives, were opposed to his politics and were unwilling to give his wife a permanent appointment on the staff. It took her a year to obtain an acting post and she had to wait until 1937 when the headmistress, Lucy Brown, took the bold step of appointing her permanently on the staff.[3]

When Grace went back to work, Tom was four years old and she worried about leaving him at home. Fortunately, she was able to enter him the following year as a pupil at the Ursuline Convent. There his hours were not exacting and he would be taken the short distance to St Michael's to wait for his mother. He became a familiar figure at the school where he aroused the maternal instincts of the girls who remembered how precarious had been his entry into the world. He was still, in the words of one of them, their special baby.[4]

The girls were drawn to him not only by his delicate

looks but by the love and esteem in which they held his mother. If Grace had reason from time to time to reprimand any of them, her reprimands, in the words of a former student, were 'always so beautifully embroidered with terms of endearment' that they were accepted cheerfully and with gratitude.[5] Moreover, the girls had more than an inkling of the stresses she had to endure with a husband as controversial as Grantley and a son as delicate as Tom.

3

The year 1937 saw her position at St Michael's stabilised, yet it was in many respects a trying time for Grace and her son. Ominous clouds were looming on the Caribbean horizon and in July the dark tempest that had been lowering overhead struck the island of Barbados. While Grantley rode the storm with unfaltering courage, it was to bring much distress to his wife and his son. Hired hooligans drove around the circular gardens at Tyrol Cot and fired shots into the house while passing policemen, not to be outdone, did the same thing from the road outside.[6]

On such occasions, Grace would take her son, then only 5 years old, to the basement of the house where they could sleep with some feeling of security. More often than not, Grace would be alone with her child, for Grantley would frequently be out in the field, not trying to fan the flames of discontent, as his detractors assumed, but to restore peace to a troubled land.

In spite of the hazards of his early years, Tom managed by the time he reached the age of 7 to find ways and means of enjoying himself. He made friends with a number of boys and girls who lived further down Spooners Hill — Tyrol Cot was at the top of that steep incline. He was allowed to use a section of the basement under the house for a club he formed. Tom made himself 'minister of finance' and each member of the club had to pay a penny (two cents) a week to retain his membership. Those who could afford it were expected to pay the princely sum of six cents a week. With these funds, members bought what ingredients they could and they cooked mainly soups on a stove provided by Tom's mother. The chief cooks were Tom and Nancy. The grounds of Tyrol Cot provided ample space for games such as Pan, rounders and hopscotch.[7]

Even at that time, his companions noticed that Tom was fascinated by postage stamps and tried to convince them that they provided 'the world's greatest picture chronicle'. Already he began to show his powers of persuasion and succeeded in involving members in what interested him. He was the one who thought of things to do and, according to Nancy, 'swiftly and easily lured his companions into joining in.' Not the least of his interests was playacting, in which he and Phyllis, the girl next door, spent most of their time.

There were times, however, when the club members found their leader domineering. Indeed, on one occasion they mutinied and there was a fight between Tom and Nancy in the basement of Tyrol Cot. Nancy emerged from the battle 'panting and victorious'. Her exhilaration was shortlived, however, for when she looked up she saw Grantley, who had entered the club room. She was horrified at being discovered thrashing Mr Adams' only son in his own house. She was vastly relieved, however, when Grantley remarked, with a grin, that he was glad that someone could control Tom.[8]

4

One year later, Tom, then nearing his eighth year, was admitted as a pupil at Harrison College. His health

6

was still a source of worry to his mother. More than once he missed a whole term owing to illness. Grace called St Elmo (now Dr) Thompson and asked him to coach her son; St Elmo readily agreed and had no difficulty in keeping Tom abreast of his studies, since he found him precociously intelligent.

When St Elmo left Barbados to join the Canadian Army in 1941, Grace had to look for another tutor to take his place, for Tom's health was a continuing problem. She soon found a substitute in C.A. (now Sir Carlisle) Burton, who visited Tyrol Cot regularly when Tom was forced by ill-health to be absent from school for long periods during term-time. Like St Elmo, Carlisle, who was then teaching at Harrison College, found it an easy task to keep Tom up-to-date in the class-work he missed during long intervals of illness.

Before long Grantley began to employ methods that were a bit different from those used by Grace. It was his task to take Tom to school every morning. In view of the many responsibilities that were now crowding in upon him, Grantley could never be sure of getting his son to school in time for morning assembly. One day he was later than usual and Tom, who was then about 9 years old, ventured to protest gently that he would be punished for arriving late. He might be put in detention. His father answered gruffly that he might be flogged and that would do him no harm. Tom sat back in his seat, seemingly petrified by the thought of the terrors that might be awaiting him in the Head-master's office. Obviously, Grantley considered it was time to toughen his son to meet the challenges of life.

Gradually, as he drew near his early teens, Tom's health began to improve. The days of the basement club were now over. Tom moved easily from his middle-class friends of that club to youngsters who were less highly placed in society. Among the lads of the neigh-bouring village he found more satisfaction in the sturdier pursuits they followed. His mother rejoiced when he started roaming through the village and joining in the games the children of the poor played in the immediate neighbourhood. He was 'Tom' to one and all and was a welcome guest at all the parties and weddings held in the area. It was here that he acquired the common touch that remained with him throughout his life.[9]

Making friends of boys further away, Tom formed a cricket team and gave them the name of the 'Arabs'. He and his fellow Arabs played matches with rivals a few miles further north in Jackson. His group had fortunately by now outgrown the dangerous pastime of coasting down the steep, constantly curving Spooners Hill in their makeshift boxcarts and scooters 'without benefit of brakes and the minimum of steering power'.[10]

That pastime had been strictly forbidden by Tom's parents. Yet it had continued for a while until it was stopped on a memorable occasion. The Arabs, after speeding down Spooners Hill, pushed their vehicles wearily up the hill. They managed to reach Tyrol Cot and its garage only to find that M820, Grantley's car, was already installed. Tom knew what to expect for defying one of the few rules imposed on him and his friends. He therefore decided to flee and did not return until he felt his defiance could be explained away by soft words.[11] From this time Tom and his companions devoted themselves more seriously to cricket and football.

_____ 5 _____

Though he found time to enjoy his many friendships, Tom was fully aware of the signs of the times. He began to pay visits to meetings of the House of Assembly to follow the discussions on the issues of the day. He grew closer to his father as he became more and more aware of the cause he was championing. He was fascinated by the Homeric battles that were fought between his father and the Attorney-General, Edward Keith Walcott, who was the principal representative of the Executive in the House and dominated the affairs of government.

If he inherited his political flair from his father, he was also indebted to him for his love of cricket. His health, though improved, was never sufficiently robust to make him proficient in the game. But he followed it with keen interest and described himself as a great spectator. Indeed, with his retentive memory he was soon established as a notable historian of the game.

He devoted himself specially to mathematics, but his schoolmates were impressed by his wide reading, his special love of literature and history and his insatiable thirst for knowledge generally. Of special note was his appreciation of the Bible and he would often seek to instruct and delight his youthful audience by quoting passages whose truth and beauty obviously enthralled him. This knowledge he was later to use on the political platform to the edification and the enjoyment of the populace.

Even at school, he showed an impressive mastery of the English language and this, added to his intellectual powers, gave him a gift for oratory that was not easily surpassed. According to a contemporary, his debating skills were first developed in the hall of Harrison College where the Acton Club held its meetings.[12]

Among his varied activities was his editorship of a mathematics magazine, the *Mathematics Announcer*. Tom took his duties as editor very seriously. Articles that were submitted by fellow-students were then handwritten by him and meticulously set out in columns. His aim was to give the layout as much authenticity as possible. Since there were no duplicators in those days, only one copy of the magazine was produced, circulated among members of the Maths Sixth and then carefully filed away in the Mathematics library.[13]

Not surprisingly, Tom was Proxime Accessit in the Barbados Scholarship in 1949, winning the Hawkins Memorial Prize; and in the following year he won the Scholarship in Mathematics. His contemporaries shared the view of the Headmaster, John Hammond, that he could have won the Scholarship in any of the major branches of study — Classics, Science or Modern Studies.

Winning a Barbados Scholarship enabled him to follow in his father's footsteps by going to the University of Oxford. Here he began the really serious preparation for the career he was to follow in later life. In view of what lay ahead of him, he could have made no better choice than the study of Politics, Philosophy and Economics.

As he left Barbados and looked back on his early life, he remembered the inspiration he drew from his father's career in the social, political and constitutional life of the island. But his heart was warmed when he recalled how his mother had guided him through the delicate stages of his life and brought his talents to healthy and happy fruition.

Notes

1. Hansard, Senate Debates, (Official Report) Enid Lynch, 18 March 1985, p. 676.
2. Letter from M.T.G. Mahon, Secretary of the Board of Education, 1 Dec. 1939.
3. Lady Adams to the author.
4. Senator Enid Lynch, Hansard, 18 March 1985, p. 676.
5. Hansard, 18 March 1985, p. 676.
6. Lady Adams to the author.
7. Gloria Cummins and Pat Symmonds, *A Personal Appreciation of J.M. G.M. Tom Adams* (unpublished), p. 6.
8. Ibid. pp. 6–7.
9. Hansard, L.L. Sisnett, 18 March, 1985, p. 2095.
10. Cummins and Symmonds, op. cit. p. 7.
11. Ibid., op. cit. pp. 7–8.
12. Henry Forde in the Memorial Issue of the *Harrisonian* n.d.
13. Ibid.

TWO

Oxford

1

While Tom was still at Harrison College his health had
almost ceased to be the wretched thing it had been in
his earlier years. In the words of one of his teachers,
even then he walked tall among his contemporaries,
was energetic, high-spirited to the point of mischief
and imbued with an intellectual curiosity that he displayed to the end of his life.[1]

When he arrived at Oxford, he was struck, like his
father before him, with the ancient magnificence of
the university. He savoured the soft autumn air that
breathed through the medieval places and was stirred
with an exhilarating sense of intellectual vitality.

Tom was to have a happier entry into Oxford than
his father. Grantley was a non-collegiate student of St
Catherine's Society and had to live in digs in Bartlemas
Road. His son, however, was enrolled as a member of
Magdalen College, that ancient society which had pro-
duced presidents, archbishops and poets.

The spirit of Magdalen is illustrated by the story
told of Sir Henry Warren, a former President of the
College. When he was interviewing a youngster who
wished to be admitted as a student of that hallowed
institution, he spoke to him as follows: 'Tell me, young
man, how do you wish to be addressed?' 'Sir,' replied the would-be student, who was a brother of the

Emperor Hirohito of Japan, 'you may address me as Your Imperial Highness, or if you prefer, as Your Royal Highness, but, as you know, in Japan I am usually referred to as the Son of God.' 'No problem with that,' replied Sir Henry. 'Magdalen has always attracted the sons of distinguished people.'

The fellow Oxonian who repeated this story for the benefit of Barbadian readers added, with a slightly picaresque touch, that Tom, as the son of so distinguished a father as Sir Grantley Adams, was no less qualified to enter the portals of Magdalen.[2]

2

Tom was appropriately impressed by the original buildings of the college that had survived almost untouched by the ravages of time and man. He felt at times as if he had slipped through the centuries and become a student of the Middle Ages.

He noted the Great Quadrangle with its cloisters and alleys, and its external windows inserted in the bays of all but one of these cloisters; the Founder's Tower of four storeys, with an embattled parapet, and the ground floor providing a gate-house of the great quadrangle; the Bell Tower, consisting of four storeys and five external stages, standing on a moulded plinth, with octagonal buttresses at each angle; the Chapel forming the south-west angle of the Great Quadrangle, with its choir of boys; and a parapet decorated with grotesque carvings of beasts and foliage; the Great Hall, with its moulded jambs and four-centred arch in a square head, and with spandrels containing shields of the arms of the College; and the President's Lodging with an embattled wall rising high above the building and continuing in a northerly direction as a towering garden wall.[3]

He was fascinated by the River Cherwell which rose far up in the Midlands with an affluent that reached to distant parts of Southern England. He knew the charms that adorned the Oxford countryside, with its still unravished landscape. It was characteristic of him that he turned to practical advantage his knowledge of the medieval grandeur of Magdalen and its sister colleges and of the glory of the Oxford countryside with its valleys, its uplands and its streams. He took American visitors on tours of the Oxford he knew so well and quite placidly accepted whatever tips were offered him. With this source of finance to augment his modest allowances from his Barbados Scholarship he was able to entertain the friends he gathered around him. And he particularly welcomed the opportunity to entertain the young ladies who were attracted by his irresistible charm.[4]

This is not to say that he was completely overwhelmed by the splendour of Magdalen and the dreaming spires of Oxford. Yet he did acquire a lasting loyalty to the ancient society of which he now became a member. He had no desire to float lotus-like along the waters of the Cherwell which bordered Magdalen. Instead, he was eager to pass through the gateway that led to High Street and to acquaint himself with the delights that arose from that busy thoroughfare. Soon he could be accounted a member of that coterie who believed that the sun rose over Magdalen and set over Worcester.

Tom's health, though improved, was not robust enough at first to withstand the vagaries of the English weather. At times he considered that the weather was 'abominable'. He was seldom free from coughs and colds and at times suffered from gastric flu and dermatitis. After spending a year in residence at Magdalen, he moved, as was the custom then and now, to digs outside the College.

'I am comfortable at 5 Pusey Street', he wrote, 'and

the exercise of walking down to College does me good. The health is absolutely splendid, but I find more and more that I need over eight hours sleep at night. Still Lord Salisbury did it every night, preferably nine, and he was Prime Minister three times.'5

—————————— 3 ——————————

Tom understood the feelings of those who regretted that the clamour of the outer world was at the gates of the ancient university. He sympathised with those who feared that the almost monastic places were on the verge of losing their idioms. Yet he shared the high spirits of the young men of his time who delighted in their health and strength.

Among those whose companionship he enjoyed was Fabian Holder, Barbados Scholar of 1948 and then at Oriel College. They had sat next to each other in the fifth and sixth forms at Harrison College and had worked to produce the college magazine. But his circle of friends was by no means limited to his classmates and Barbadians. It included Hector Wynter, Emile George, Asquith Phillips, George Moe, Denys and Colin Williams, Eddie Brathwaite and Ken Woods, who later served with him at the BBC.

Soon his interests extended further afield. He played an active part in the politics of West Indian students. He became a member of the Oxford Labour Party and made contacts with some of the leading political figures of the day. In spite of all these interests and activities, Tom found time to read his course of Politics, Philosophy and Economics. He never seemed preoccupied with his studies, relying on his quick brain and retentive memory to get him through the required reading in the minimum of time. Not surprisingly, he won only third-class honours at the end of the Trinity Term in 1954. He gained his BA in November 1954, proceeding to the degree of MA in July 1958.[6]

If he did not win high academic honours, he gained valuable experience by meeting men like Hugh Gaitskell and Creech Jones and women like Shirley Williams, to all of whom he was soon familiarly known as Tom. He possessed the gift of mixing with such celebrities as easily as he had done with the poor children in the neighbourhood of Tyrol Cot. He canvassed for the British Labour Party at election time and during the Party Conference in Blackpool in 1952 he served as an unofficial Personal Assistant to Gaitskell.

4

In view of his poor health during childhood and his cardiac problem in later years, Tom Adams could scarcely have survived as long as he did without his gift for relaxation. One of the main hobbies that helped to ease the stresses of his career was stamp collecting.

We have seen that Tom at the age of seven was already interested in this hobby. His ardour as a philatelist was increased by his longstanding friendship with Stuart Spalding who was an Oxford lecturer and a renowned figure in the world of philately to which he gave more than 70 years of his life. During his long life he made many friends as a stamp collector and among these he was proud to number Tom Adams.[7]

When Spalding returned from the war in 1946, he wrote to graduates of St Catherine's, Oxford, and asked if they would exchange stamps with him. That is how he met Grantley who passed him on to Tom who became one of his correspondents.

Five years later when Tom entered Magdalen, Grantley asked Spalding to keep a fatherly eye on him. Their main interest was that Spalding lectured in politics and economics and Tom was one of his students; but while the lecturer's interest was academic, that of the student was more of a consuming personal enthusiasm.

Politics, economics and philately made the two men close friends. No matter how outrageous the lecturer's political arguments were at times, Tom took them all in good faith. Sometimes when the student admitted the lecturer was right, the latter would respond that he (Tom) was becoming a real politician.[8]

Tom spent most of his holidays with the lecturer's family in Lowestoft. He made many friends there of all types, Spalding added. The latter noticed that Tom was a sociable person and he feared that his student might become more fond of socialising than of academic work. His fear in this respect, he later noted, proved to be unfounded.

Tom impressed Spalding with his self-control, particularly when he came across the odd case of colour prejudice. He would be obviously perturbed by it but never showed resentment or animosity. Spalding was impressed that Tom reacted in a dignified manner. It seems that on the whole he was cordially received and invited to all sorts of parties, especially by the young ladies of the Magdalen staff.

After he left Magdalen for London, he continued his visits to Spalding and his little circle at Lowestoft; and when Tom married, he brought his newly-wed wife to see the old gentleman. Some years later when Spalding came to Barbados he was the guest of his former student. The two men were drawn together not only by their academic disciplines but by their interest in philately, each helping to enrich the collection of the other. Before the end, Tom had the best stamp collection in Barbados and perhaps in the English-speaking Caribbean.

Little did Spalding know that Tom was destined to share the fate of another Oxonian who was, like him, the son of a Prime Minister. Tom Adams, like Raymond Asquith, was showered by the good fairies with many gifts. As Spalding would have agreed, they both enjoyed a handsome presence, a gift of persuasive eloquence, an intellect that swiftly absorbed whatever attracted its attention, a consuming interest in things of the mind and spirit, and a personality that made them accessible to the highest and the lowest. Richly dowered they undoubtedly were, but there was one thing they were both denied — length of years.

When Tom died, no one mourned more deeply than the man who had introduced him at Oxford to the intricacies of politics and economics and had for many years shared with him a love of the fascinating world of philately.

In 1954, however, Tom was in no mood to entertain morbid thoughts of the future. He never sought to be a 'professional student'.[9] He had spent three idyllic years at Oxford, enjoying undergraduate life to the full. He had continued the preparation for the world of politics which he had already started in his home at Tyrol Cot. Now he turned his face to London where he would pursue the study of law and explore the wider stages of life.

Notes

1. Professor Sir Roy Marshall, at Westminster Abbey, 23 May 1985.
2. Cameron, later Sir James Tudor, *Barbados Advocate*, 17 March, 1985.
3. Confirmed by the author's personal observation during a visit to Magdalen in August 1986, some 35 years after Tom's stay at the College.
4. Related by Lady Adams to the author, 15 Jan. 1986.
5. Letter to his mother, 25 June 1953.
6. From Mrs B. Parry Jones, Archivist, Magdalen College.
7. Letter to Lady Adams from Spalding, 8 March 1987.
8. Ibid.
9. Letter to his mother, 10 Dec. 1954.

THREE

London

When Tom left Magdalen, he walked into High Street for the last time as a student and passed through the gateway that led to London. He may well have felt as if he was leaving a woman of enchanting beauty who had cast a spell on him; a creature in whose soul there was nothing cheap or tawdry; a spirit that possessed the knowledge of almost everything that can happen to a human being.

Yet, with his unfailing high spirits, he was prepared to face the challenge of London. He was never daunted by the feeling that he was an insignificant unit among the metropolitan millions of the big city.

Actually, he had already had wide experiences by his travels outside the United Kingdom. After winning on the football pools in 1952, he spent some time in Ireland where 'living was cheap and food was plentiful.'[1] The following year he visited Paris and was enthralled by the many-sided attractions of that city.[2]

Tom met Genevieve at the BBC in 1957. She was the daughter of Philip Turner who was at the time Chairman of the Civil Service Legal Society. He had served in the Second World War as an officer in the Royal Navy. After the war he returned to the Civil Service where he had a distinguished career, eventually becoming head of the legal department of the British

Post Office. For his meritorious work in the public service he was honoured with the award of a CBE.

Genevieve had just left school and technical college and had taken up her first job as a secretary at the BBC. At that time Tom was a freelance writer and producer with the Caribbean Service. In the years that followed she met Sir Grantley and Norman Manley and was charmed with their old-world courtesies. She and Tom used to have dinner with them at the old Charing Cross Hotel which seemed to her in those days to be a place of surpassing grandeur.

It was after he met Genevieve that Tom paid a visit to Moscow which he described as 'a pleasant enough city', although everything had 'an old-fashioned appearance'. The skyscrapers looked out of date, as did the blocks of flats and the shops. To him there were far too many wooden shacks and the weather was 'vile'.[3] But he could not fail to be impressed by the University, the Kremlin, the Bolshoi, the Sparrow Hills (renamed Lenin Hills) and not the least a bus which had been driven from Oxford in all 'its London double-decked glory'.[4] One thing he specially liked in Russia was the food.

Tom took an impish delight in imagining the thrill of the Post Office people in Barbados when they saw all his letters and postcards arriving from Russia with their unmistakeable Soviet stamps.[5]

After his return from Russia, Genevieve and Tom went together to the Russian Exhibition at Earls Court. Genevieve recalls that it was the same year that Yuri Gargarin first went into space and they celebrated the occasion by treating themselves to good Russian food.[6]

2

His father before him held the considered opinion that the education in the Classics he had received at

Harrison College and Oxford should be supplemented by a rigorous training in an exact science like the law. His son did not disagree. Tom's mathematical training at Harrison College was to prove of great value throughout his life. His study at Oxford of politics, philosophy and economics was to prepare him for the career that lay ahead of him in Barbados. His training in law gave him an increased interest in the precise meaning of words and later enabled him to deal with obtuse juries, captious judges and obscurantist politicians. And, not the least, his experience with the BBC taught him the value of the electronic media and was to make him, in due course, the great communicator in the public life of Barbados.

Tom followed his father's example by enrolling as a student of Gray's Inn. He was fascinated by the history of law, by the principles that were laid down by the great jurists of the past, by the gaiety and friendliness of the Inns of Court and the procedures of the Bar and the Bench. He did not, however, overly exert himself as an assiduous student. As at Oxford, so at Gray's Inn, he relied on his quick intellect and his retentive memory to get him through his Bar examinations with a minimum of effort. He did, however, get a Class II in his law finals. There were no Class I successes in his section and the only other Class II was obtained by a Gray's Inn man.

Politics continued to attract him in London as it had done at Oxford. As before, he associated with leading members of the British Labour Party, particularly with his Oxford contemporary, Shirley Williams, then an adherent of that Party, but now a prominent member of the Social Democratic Party. He worked in the East End of London to help the underprivileged and campaigned for the BLP whenever he considered his services were needed.

Tom's involvement in the W.I. Student Centre at

Earls Court is indicated by his election first as Secretary and later as Vice-President of the Centre. It is significant that he was never elected President there. According to George Stoll, who knew him from Oxford days, and while he was in London, and kept in touch with him until the time of his death in 1985, there were several reasons for this. First, it was held against him that his father had made the 'infamous' speech at the UN meeting in Paris in 1948 defending the British Labour Government's colonial policy against Soviet Russia. Secondly, he was a man of honour who took a principled stand on all issues raised at the Centre, recking little of the consequences that might follow. Thirdly, Barbadian students were in the minority in the Centre and he had to canvas the support of other West Indians, mainly Jamaicans.[7]

Yet Tom never gave up. He devoted more and more of his energy to the Centre where he played a prominent part in the at-times tempestuous politics of the day. He was at the centre of every controversy. Here perhaps more than at Oxford, he developed the attributes of the political animal. And while he never won the complete popularity he deserved, the students of all parts of the WI knew that when they were in trouble, they could turn to him for help, in view of his knowledge and expertise in the law.[8]

3

George Stoll and Tom were drawn together by their interest in cricket and bridge. The latter, he asserted, was more challenging to a man's wits than poker. He remembered playing bridge with Tom, when he had free evenings, as often as five times a week, while poker was played during the weekends. He expressed regret that not a few in Barbados failed to distinguish between Tom's keen interest in bridge and his so-called addiction to poker.[9]

Tom served with the BBC from 1957 to 1962. Through his influence as producer of the West Indian Service he was able to help many of his compatriots who happened to be in sore financial straits. Indeed, it is no exaggeration to say that he played no little part in helping to establish the BBC as a patron of the arts.

Among those with whom he worked were George Steadman, Ulric Cross, Jerry Mansell and Douglas Muggeridge, with whom he was to form lasting friend-ships. Others whose work he enjoyed and whose writings he encouraged were Sam Selvon, George Lamming, V.S. Naipaul and Andrew Salkey. In view of his consuming interest in cricket, he inevitably became very friendly with Bertie Clarke. And his many-sided activities at the WI Student Centre made him a close friend of Winston 'Pony' Hynam.

After their engagement, Tom talked to Genevieve about his association with the British Labour Party and took her to the settlement in the East End where he worked for the Party. Every Christmas he used to work in the sorting section of the Post Office to make extra money when he was a student at Gray's Inn.

They knew each other for four and a half years before they were married. Unfortunately, Genevieve used to work in London during the week and spend the weekends at home with her family in Epsom, Surrey. It meant catching early trains in those days to get home and Tom was able to take her to Surrey only during the brief period when he owned a very ancient car.

The result of this was that Genevieve never really got into his 'crowd' and certainly never met any of his more 'disreputable' friends who initiated him in the practice of playing bridge and poker for whole weekends at a time.

With his mother, Grace, when he had just entered the Ursuline Convent School.

Tom at 9, a pupil of Harrison College.

Tyrol Cot, Tom's childhood home.

The Oxford graduate.

In an East End Settlement, London, early 1950s.

At the BBC Tom was one of the producers of the daily programme *Calling the Caribbean* and was responsible for the programme *West Indians Over Here*, and programmes for women.

With his fiancée.

Gray's Inn Chapel: a new bride and groom.

Tom, Genevieve and Douglas, 1964.

Tom and Genevieve were married in Gray's Inn Chapel on 2 June 1962, and George Stoll was his best man. 'He always said that ours was the best wedding he ever went to and that it was the happiest day of his life. And, of course, Tom the romantic took us to Venice for our honeymoon which was also a perfect time for us both.'[10]

Genevieve remembered the months that followed their wedding as among the happiest of both their lives. Tom worked in Dingle Foot's chambers in Gray's Inn for six months after their marriage and before he returned to Barbados. It was an experience that added to his preparation for the work that lay ahead of him. He had now been in London for ten years and away from Barbados for thirteen years. When asked when he would ever return to his native land, he would reply facetiously that Barbados was not big enough to accommodate two Adamses at once.

During the last six months in London Tom made serious preparations for his return to the island. It was a sort of climax of his efforts to equip himself for what he knew lay ahead of him. No one was better qualified to speak of this than Henry Forde, who remembered the warmth of his friendship during their joint student days in London.

Tom's house at 47 Nevern Square, SW 5 in the Earls Court area, was open to all and sundry and Henry admitted that many of his friends misused that freedom. 'Whether it was another student colleague from Oxford days, or whether it was "York" Marryshow, the son of a great West Indian who had come on lean financial days, Tom Adams was always willing to assist. Many of us therefore took his generosity, his time, his warmth and his friendship for granted.'[11]

Henry Forde then proceeded to speak of the ways in

which Tom had qualified himself for a career in politics. 'During his days at Oxford, he had become a legend for organisation on the political level, whether it was the student politics of the Oxford Union or assisting in the Oxford Labour Party. When he came to London, that same meticulous care was evident when he participated in the politics of the West Indian Students' Centre. But he always found time for friendship, and I remember him as perhaps the most consummate host that one could ever have. When he entertained you he saw to every detail. He made sure that you were happy and relaxed, he catered to your taste, and you felt at home with him.'[12]

When Tom returned to Barbados he seemed prepared to face whatever lay before him and he certainly had no fear of what his fate would be.

Notes

1. Letter to Mum and Dad, Good Friday, 1952.
2. Letter to Mum and Dad, 25 Aug. 1953.
3. Letter to 'Mama and Papa', 29 Sept. 1958.
4. Ibid.
5. Letter from Genevieve to the author, 19 April 1987.
6. Letter from Tom to 'Mama and Papa', 29 Sept. 1958.
7. Author's interview with George Stoll in London, 15 Aug. 1986.
8. Ibid.
9. Ibid.
10. Letter from Genevieve to the author, 1 July 1985.
11. Henry Forde, Hansard, 18 March 1985, p. 2085.
12. Ibid.

FOUR

Father and Son

1

In January 1963, accompanied by his wife, Tom left London deep in snow and set out for the tropical warmth of his native land. In May of that year, their son Douglas was born and four years later a second son, Rawdon, arrived on the scene as another Barbadian.

At first they took up temporary residence at Tyrol Cot, where they stayed for 15 months. Tyrol Cot was full of many memories for the Adams family. For it was here that Sir Grantley had brought his wife, Grace, after their marriage in 1929. It was here that Tom had spent the first twenty years of his life. He had always been impressed with the design of the house, distinguished with its elongated Roman arches. His years of absence had not dimmed the impression it had made on him from his childhood days. Tyrol Cot to him was not a house but a home, conveying 'a sense of period and purpose'. It was 'a place with an instinct for gracious living, a love of beautiful things, an aura of lives lived richly, in the fullest sense.'[1]

Tom remembered Tyrol Cot as a house that had been built in the spacious days of the past, with its high ceilings, its curious window shutters and window seats, its galleries, its drawing and dining rooms, and its external walls all conceived and constructed in classical proportions.[2]

There to welcome Tom again was his mother's fine collection of blue Wedgwood, which decorated the dining room, his father's selection of African mementoes and his choice of British Museum reproductions displayed on the walls near the front door.

To this gracious residence had been welcomed the outstanding figures of the Caribbean — Norman Manley, Sir John Mordecai, Albert Marryshow, Sir Hugh Wooding, Phyllis Allfrey, Albert Thorne, Robert Bradshaw, Vere Bird, Lord Hailes, Nigel Fisher and Ronald Tree. Tom particularly remembered the distinguished Africans who visited from time to time. But he had a special reason to recall the visit of the Royal Commission, notably the trade unionists, Sir Walter Citrine and Morgan Jones. For, when these came to dinner one evening, Tom was allowed, although only eight years old at the time, to sit at the table with them on the condition that he remained as unobtrusive as possible.

At one point, however, the question of the suffragette movement was raised and there was some hesitation to answer the query when that movement was started. Tom at once blurted out the correct date and continued to give some additional information about the movement. When the audience stared at him in astonishment, he was immediately reduced to an embarrassed silence.[3]

2

Strange as it may seem, harmony did not prevail for long after Tom's return to Tyrol Cot. Soon there were frequent discussions and arguments between father and son. They were both strong men who had been trained in the disputatious atmosphere of the Inns of Court. They argued on almost every conceivable subject and Grace was frequently consumed with worry that the two men she dearly loved did not seem to get on well together while they lived under the same roof. What intrigued her was that the more they argued the better they ate and the more soundly they slept.

Eventually, things came to a climax over a minor incident. Sir Grantley used to say that he was a radical in politics but a conservative in dress.[4] One got the impression that this remark was made as much in seriousness as in jest. This proved to be the case on one occasion when he and Grace were in their car about to set out to see a cricket match at Kensington Oval. Just before he drove off, Tom jumped into the back seat, dressed only in shirt and pants. His father at once made it clear that his son would not be coming with them to cricket unless he was properly attired with a jacket and collar and tie.

When his father refused to give way on his point, Tom got out of the car, slammed the door and made his way to the phone. He rang the present writer and asked if he could come to see me. He emphasised that he wanted to see me immediately. While he was on his way to my house in Maxwell, Genevieve rang me, saying that she had never seen Tom so angry and agitated; and she expressed the hope that some words could be found to appease his wrath and soothe his spirit.

When Tom arrived, we spoke for hours. He said his father kept pressing him to enter politics. He did not agree because the two of them were always arguing and he feared that their quarrels, which were then private, would become public. The conversation between us was largely a one-sided one. I listened in silence for the most part, though I thought I knew what the cause of the dispute was between father and son.

The Barbados Labour Party had recently suffered a

crushing defeat at the hands of the Democratic Labour Party. That was in 1961. The following year saw the inglorious death of the WI Federation of which Sir Grantley had been Prime Minister during the four years of its existence. He had known the ecstasy of its inauguration and the agony of its dissolution. He was anxious to rebuild the BLP as the basis on which the regional movement could be reconstructed.

On the other hand, Tom, whose practice at the Bar was only modest, wanted to establish his family first. Shrewd calculator that he always was, he knew that as the son of an illustrious father, he would find a good deal of resentment among some people who 'grudged him'.[5] It was not easy for him in such circumstances to come back to Barbados without realising that some might want to settle their scores with his father against him personally. He knew what it would mean to function *sub magni nominis umbra* — under the shadow of a great name. Yet he recognised the wider duty which he had to the people of Barbados and was soon prepared to throw himself fully into the political life of the country.[6]

3

My suggestion that he move from Tyrol Cot and establish his own home was readily accepted. With a minimum of delay he transferred his little family to 'Sunset' in Enterprise Road, Christ Church.

Genevieve did not have an easy life in Barbados because of all the new things she had to adjust to. Not the least of these were the uncertainties and hazards of politics. Yet she could recall that her life was full, happy, exciting and interesting. Looking back after a period of more than twenty years, she could never forget that she had married an extraordinary and loving man.[7]

What made him such a person was 'the fact that he loved absolutely everything in life and did 90 percent of it better than most other people. He was always fun, never boring, and above all a tremendous worker and fighter and able to make things happen and other people achieve what they never would have done otherwise. But his breadth as a human being I feel, is vital because it is really that that gave him his brilliance as a political leader.'[8]

Nor was this all. In the years ahead, Genevieve discovered that Tom was to prove a 'very understanding father'. He found time on Saturdays to take their two sons, Douglas and Rawdon, to the beach at Brighton.

The boys owned a boat and their father went out to sea with them. Tom seldom, if ever, used force with them, relying instead on gentle persuasion. He treated them often by taking them out to meals. He confided in them and they usually knew what he was doing. One day, for example, their grandmother phoned to ask to speak to Tom, and Rawdon answered, 'Daddy has gone to play poker.'[9]

Genevieve, herself an accomplished pianist and keen dancer, came from a musical family. This gift she passed on to her sons who learned music and both became quite good pianists. They were encouraged to develop their talent by being given several musical instruments.[10]

Tom added variety to a gifted family by being a good cook, especially of Chinese food. To improve his cooking he bought and read books on cookery.

The marriage of Genevieve and Tom was turbulent but it certainly was not an unhappy one. She always insisted, firmly and with conviction, that their relationship was strong and close and that they cared very much for each other. Certainly, she never lost sight of the qualities that won her love and admiration from the time she left school and technical college.[11]

4

The change from Tyrol Cot to Sunset, Enterprise Road, proved to be one of the happy things that resulted from a well-remembered conversation between Tom and myself. The removal of constant pressures and the absence of almost unending disputes and squabbles worked like a charm in the sense that it brought father and son together again. It was once again like the youthful days at Tyrol Cot and the frequent meetings in London when father and son were inseparables.

Now they worked together, tending the gardens of Tyrol Cot and planning to rebuild the Barbados Labour Party. They were resolved to restore it to the status it enjoyed in former times. The matter of formal or informal wear was completely forgotten. Tom became as conservative in dress as his father had been. He dressed with immaculate taste — a practice that increased his almost irresistible charm with the ladies. His reputation in this area grew with the years as his influence in the island increased.

'He was tall and handsome,' the author was once told. 'He had manners and was always well groomed. He had money and position. The female of the species solicited him on all sides. Great respect Sir; but have you never heard of John F. Kennedy?'[12]

Actually, Tom had no money in his earlier years to influence anyone. When he and his wife arrived in Barbados, they almost literally had nothing. Many of the arguments with Sir Grantley in the early days had been about money, because he had hoped he would go into practice with his father. But the latter was too preoccupied with the condition of the Barbados Labour Party to think of returning to the Bar.[13]

Instead, Tom had to rent an office and all that went with it, on his own. He really needed financial help from his father. So hard pressed were the young couple that Genevieve had to go out to work six weeks after Douglas was born. Everything that Tom ever had he worked 'jolly hard' for and so did Genevieve. The report that he was rich was just another myth.[14]

As the years passed his early arguments with his father became dim memories. He would recall with profound agreement, many of the things Sir Grantley used to say on Barbadian and West Indian affairs. Indeed, as a shrewd commentator had noted, he took the fact that he was his father's son very seriously. He frequently referred in his conversation to the comments his father used to make and the advice he offered on critical occasions. Nor did he forget those who had helped Sir Grantley in his pioneer work and took advantage of every opportunity to include them in the various Honours Lists in recognition of the service they had given their country at a crucial time.[15] Some of these he even recommended for the accolade of knighthood — Sir Deighton Ward, Sir Mencea Cox, Sir MacDonald Blunt, Sir Kenneth Hunte, Sir Edwy Talma, Sir Ronald Mapp and the present writer. Nita Barrow and Elsie Payne were appointed to the Order of Barbados in the grade of Dame of St Andrew because he recognised their services to the community as a whole and to the outside world.

His respect and admiration for his father grew as the years went by. It was written, at the time of his death, that he most certainly conceived it his duty to push on to reality the dreams his father passed on to him. He did not need to be reminded that one of those dreams was a union of the West Indies and that his father had the horrid responsibility to preside over its dismantling. To put the broken bits together has been described as the most challenging of his inheritances and it is one of the tragedies of our time that he did not live long enough to meet that daunting challenge.[16]

Notes

1. Address by Dame Elsie Payne, 29 April 1978.
2. Ibid.
3. Related to the author by Lady Adams, 1 Oct. 1976, and recalled in the *Bajan Magazine*, March 1985.
4. Sir Grantley to the author on more than one occasion.
5. Henry Forde, Hansard, 18 March 1985, p. 2085.
6. Ibid.
7. Letter from Genevieve Adams to the author, 19 April 1987.
8. Letter from Genevieve to the author, 1 July 1985.
9. Communicated to the author by Lady Adams.
10. Letter from Genevieve to the author, 19 April 1987.
11. Letter from Genevieve to the author, 1 July 1985.
12. A.K. 'Dick' Walcott to the author, 9 June 1986.
13. Letter from Genevieve to the author, 19 April 1987.
14. Ibid.
15. Senator John Wickham, the *Sunday Sun*, 17 March 1985.
16. Ibid.

FIVE

Into the Arena

1

When Tom Adams returned to Barbados, he found a social climate that was vastly different from what it had been in the years when he was growing up in Tyrol Cot. He passed from childhood to early manhood when the politics of a newly emerging Barbados radiated from his home and left an indelible influence on his views. He was six years old when the upheaval of 1937 took place, with the poor and the disadvantaged protesting violently against the hardships and privation they endured.

He remembered the vibrant atmosphere that pervaded the island when Clement Payne, with proselytising zeal, preached the gospel of trade unionism in Barbados. He recalled how his father was drawn into the movement and was regarded as the fountain and origin of the disturbances and the explosive conditions that followed. Nor could he forget the attempt to burn down Tyrol Cot, the protection provided by the workers who encircled the grounds with 'pill-boxes', the police who patrolled the street and fired occasional shots near the house, the loving care of his mother who slept with him in the basement to keep him safe while the random shooting was going on, and his father frequently absent on the business of promoting the cause of working-class organisation.[1]

By the time he had reached the age of 10, he knew what it meant when his father became the undisputed leader of the Barbados Progressive League with its two powerful offsprings, the Barbados Labour Party and the Barbados Workers Union.[2] Sir Grantley was now at the head of a monolithic movement that made him the most powerful and at the same time the busiest man in Barbados.

To Tom, during his tender years, Tyrol Cot appeared at times to be a peaceful haven over which his mother presided with dignity and an ineffable charm. Yet he was aware that from this house were to radiate the powerful influences that were to introduce a far-reaching change in the order of Barbadian society.

2

Before he left for Oxford, his father appeared to go from strength to strength. First with the help of H.W. (later Sir Hugh) Springer and later with that of Frank Walcott, he established the political ascendancy of the Barbados Labour Party and made the Barbados Workers Union a dominant force in the industrial life of the island. In 1946 he became, under the Bushe Experiment, the first Premier of Barbados. In 1947 he was elected President of the Caribbean Labour Congress and was called on by 30 000 workers assembled in the Kingston race course in Jamaica to lead the people of the Caribbean to West Indian nationhood.[3]

Tom followed other developments with equal interest. In 1948 his father entered the international field when he defended the colonial policy of the British Labour Party against Soviet Russia and incurred the criticism of left-wing critics in many parts of the world.[4] Yet in the same year he won the General Election in Barbados and formed the first Labour Government in the history of the island. The following year he was elected a member of the Executive Board of the International Confederation of Free Trade Unions. In 1950 adult suffrage was introduced into Barbados and within a year Grantley was again victorious in the General Election, winning an impressive number of seats of the House of Assembly.

Such was the situation when Tom left Barbados to enter Magdalen College, Oxford. But when he returned home early in 1963 he found that the political scene had changed almost beyond recognition. In the words of a contemporary, 'the political pendulum had swung with a vengeance. The Party, which had at first ushered in the revolutionary movement, and later laid the solid foundations for political, economic and social development, had suffered its first major defeat. It was now in Opposition. Many of its parliamentary members had lost their seats. The shining star had sunk into seemingly Stygian darkness.[5]

The political realities in 1963 would have seemed harsh and daunting to anyone less spirited than Tom. In the past the BLP and the BWU were bound together in what appeared to be an almost indissoluble union. Such organisation as existed was built around the Union and the BLP owed its existence to the personality of Grantley Adams. After 1954 the Party and the Union went their separate ways.

In 1958 when Adams went to Port-of-Spain, Trinidad, to assume the responsibilities of Prime Minister of the WI Federation, there was a definite break in the consciousness of the Barbadian people.[6] The problem that had to be settled before his departure was who should succeed him as Premier of Barbados. The choice lay between M.E. (later Sir Mencea) Cox and Dr H.G. Cummins. It was argued that, if any man in the BLP could claim a national image and display leadership qualities, it was Cox, then Acting Leader of the House.[7]

C.L.R. James thought highly of him, describing him as 'an outstanding figure, self-made, a man of ability, character and presence.[8] In the end the choice fell on Dr H.G. Cummins, whose chief claim to selection was that he was more likely than Cox to unite his Cabinet colleagues.[9]

3

While Grantley Adams departed from the political scene in 1958, Errol Barrow regained a seat in the House of Assembly as a result of a by-election in St John the same year. The Democratic Labour Party had already begun to sense the possibility of victory over the Cummins Government. With Barrow's return to the House, the Party became even sharper in its criticism of the Government and began to show more and more that it was a credible alternative to the regime of the day 'with different and even better fiscal policies.'[10]

When Tom returned to Barbados, he found the DLP firmly entrenched in power. When he moved to Enterprise Road he had more time to give undisturbed reflection to the affairs of state and the condition of the BLP. Now that he and his father were no longer living under the same roof, he meditated more frequently and more deeply on the pioneer work of the BLP and how gravely his father's activities had been underestimated not only in Barbados but in the outside world.

Paradoxical as it may seem, now that he was no longer living in Tyrol Cot he appreciated, perhaps more than before, the significance of that house in a crucial period of the island's history. He visited the house frequently to console his father in the time of his near-desolation when all his efforts to build the progressive movement in Barbados and to lead the

West Indies to nationhood had ended disastrously.

He realised that, at a time when all his father's ventures seemed to be crashing into irretrievable ruin, Grantley's spirit remained indomitable largely because of the unfailing support of the woman he had married more than thirty years previously. In spite of his removal to Sunset, Tom was frequently drawn to Tyrol Cot because he was convinced that his mother would be to him too a source of inspiration and inner strength in the course he was now resolved to follow.

For Tom had learnt much of the grim realities of politics from his experience in London. He knew what was to be expected in Barbados, within and without the BLP, from those who might resent the idea of an Adams dynasty. He was aware that there would be opposition to any easy advance to the higher levels of the Party's hierarchy. He was also not unaware of the opponents outside the Party who would strongly resent the idea of an Adams succeeding an Adams. Once again he recognised the perils of functioning *sub magni nominis umbra*.

Nevertheless, Tom was prepared by 1964 to meet the sea of troubles that would beset him, not as single spies but in battalions. He saw that the clamant need of the Party was organisation. The close links that had existed between the BLP and the Barbados Workers Union in the period 1941 to 1954, had been severed ten years before. Tom undertook the duties of Secretary in 1965 and almost from the beginning showed his attention to detail, his capacity for hard work and his flair for organisation.

4

After the disastrous general election of 1961, the BLP gave a much better performance in 1966. There were several reasons for this — Grantley Adams' return to the political fray, the numerous meetings held after 1962 and the 'windfall' issue which arose from the question as to whether to fund the unexpected money derived from the increased price of sugar or to pay it out to the workers as a special bonus. Undoubtedly, one of the factors in the improved performance of the BLP was the organisation Tom provided for the Party both island-wide and at constituency level.

In this election Tom ran for St Thomas along with Ronald Mapp in the two-member constituency system which then prevailed in the island. Mapp lost by a narrow margin. But Tom seemed his cool, confident self throughout the campaign. When asked on one occasion what were his chances of winning, he replied with his characteristic smile: 'I think I will be returned Senior Member on Election Day.'[11] And that is exactly what happened a month later.

While Tom was thrilled at winning handsomely in St Thomas, to Genevieve his victory at the top of the poll was a source of great relief. During the election campaign, his chief opponent had attacked her incessantly from the platform and she was afraid Tom might lose the seat for having married a white woman. Other opponents did use this tactic throughout his career, but it never succeeded and Tom always assured her that it would not and that she was not to worry about such attacks.[12]

A number of prominent persons lost their seats in this election. Among these were Fred Goddard, Freddie Miller, Wynter Crawford and Frank Walcott. On the other hand, in addition to Tom, another young man, Bernard St John, was elected to a seat in the Assembly. These two were to play significant roles in the fortunes of the BLP and the affairs of the country.

The results of the general election which was held on 3 November 1966, were that the DLP won 14 seats, the BLP 8 and the Barbados National Party 2. What the BLP regarded as significant was that in four of the constituencies the margin of defeat was almost minimal. In addition, the election saw the return of Sir Grantley to the House.

5

For Tom one of the most important lessons to be learnt from the 1966 election was that with better organisation, greater financial support and harder work by candidates in their constituencies, the DLP, which had won such a convincing victory five years before, might have been defeated if only by a narrow margin.[13]

It should be mentioned that in his task of organisation Tom received valuable support not only from Bernard St John but from stalwarts like M.E. Cox, R.G. Mapp, Lionel Craig, L.B. Brathwaite, Clarence Jemmott, DeLisle Bradshaw, Burton Hinds, Mrs Lorraine Payne, sister-in-law of Clement Payne, Donald ('Buckie') Seale, and Mrs Mardelle Greene. Other members were rapidly coming to the fore to assist the cause of the BLP. These and others were to work with Tom for victory in the future. But before that was achieved, there were to be many arguments and differences between Tom and those who were reluctant to follow his lead in all matters.

It has to be admitted that at an early stage Tom received so little cooperation within the Party that Genevieve felt constrained to intervene. Young, new to Barbados and very nervous, she approached St John, whom she hardly knew at the time, and besought him to use his calm, beneficent influence to help Tom against his critics at Party Committee meetings. Even Tom seemed amazed that she should have done such a thing, but she was convinced that it produced a positive result.[14] Certainly from that time a spirit of amity and comradeship existed between Adams and St John until the end.

Errol Barrow himself, with characteristic candour, expressed his disappointment not only with the defeat of Frank Walcott in St Peter, but with the general performance of his Party.[15] 'I had expected', he openly admitted, 'to get many more seats than we previously held, and I can only surmise that within the last 48 hours something had occurred in the country to cause an upset.'[16]

Actually, as indicated before, there were a number of things that caused this upset. Not the least of these was Tom's flair for organisation. Nor was it the last instance we were to see what that special gift could produce.

Notes

1. F.A. Hoyos, *The Story of the Progressive Movement* (Barbados, Second edition 1949) p. 30.
2. Ibid. pp. 11–12.
3. F.A. Hoyos, *The Rise of West Indian Democracy* (Barbados, 1964) p. 119.
4. Ibid. pp. 128–33.
5. Sir Ronald Mapp, 'Master of Political Strategy', *Nation* newspaper, 15 March 1985.
6. C.L.R. James, 'Analysis of the Political Situation in Barbados' (Private circulation), July 1958, p. 2.
7. Ibid. p. 4.
8. Ibid.
9. Ibid. p. 5.
10. Dr Richard Cheltenham, *The Political and Constitutional Development of Barbados, 1946–66* (Doctoral thesis, University of Manchester, 1970, published in Barbados by the Democratic Labour Party), p. 178.
11. Tom Adams to the author.
12. Letter from Genevieve to the author, 19 April 1987.
13. Ronald Mapp, op. cit.
14. Letter from Genevieve Adams to the author, 19 April 1987.
15. Cheltenham, op. cit. p. 261.
16. *Barbados Advocate*, 8 November 1966.

SIX

Member of Parliament

1

The election of 1966 was the last to be fought under the double-member constituency system.

Tom was exhilarated by his success but he was very disappointed that Ronald Mapp failed, by a narrow margin, to win the second seat. He knew what sacrifices Mapp had made by resigning from the public service at an early age and entering on the hazards of a political career. Tom realised how hard Mapp had worked to make the Party newspaper, the *Beacon*, an effective organ for supporting the views of the BLP and considered that no man deserved recognition for his services to the cause of the working-class movement more.

Tom was proud to enter the new House of Assembly along with his father who had been elected as a representative of his old constituency of St Joseph. Tom was well aware of the hazards he had to face. He did not want to revive the arguments he had had with his father when he first returned to Barbados. He was content to play the role of the loyal and dutiful son, content to subdue at times his own feelings.[1]

He also knew the opposition he would run into if he showed, at this time, a firm resolution to make a bid for political leadership. He was acutely conscious of the risks he would incur, arising from charges of nepotism, and feelings of rivalry and envy. Once again, he realised the hazards of living and working under the shadow of a great name.

The course Tom decided to follow in these circumstances seemed obvious to a close friend and contemporary. 'At that time, I got the impression that Tom was not particularly intent on preparing for a possible leadership role.... He seemed to be so relaxed, pursuing intently his career as a lawyer, and paying close attention to his hobbies (like his father, he was an ardent gardener), to collecting stamps and, of course, first and foremost, to looking after his wife and other members of the family.'[2]

2

The late A.K. Walcott, eldest son of the once-formidable E.K. Walcott, Attorney-General of Barbados, was asked on one occasion by his father to suggest the names of Barbadians and other West Indians who were likely to return from universities in the UK to a brilliant career in the Caribbean. Dick, as he was familiarly known, answered his father's request and mentioned, among others, the name of Henry Forde. At the time, he frankly admitted he regarded Tom Adams as a lightweight.[3]

Later when Dick was on the Bench in Barbados, he could not fail to admit Tom's legal talent. The care with which he prepared his cases and the incisive logic with which he presented them, could not fail to win Dick's admiration. The latter was no mean judge in such matters. He had won First Class Honours at Pembroke College, Cambridge, and was awarded the George Long Prize in Jurisprudence. One day, he was so impressed by Tom's performance in his Court that he went home and told his wife, Lillie, that he had just listened to the best lawyer in Barbados. When he was reminded of his pronouncement on Henry Forde as a lawyer, he replied, with the language of hyperbole he used on the rare occasions when he was deeply moved, that Tom was twice as good.[4]

While building up his practice and relaxing with his hobbies, Tom took a careful note of what was happening in the House of Assembly, especially after he had entered it as the Senior Member for St Thomas. He mastered the rules of the House, functioned carefully within its methods of procedure and gave the Speaker all the deference that was due to him.

Tom's first major speech was on the Supreme Court of Judicature Bill. He submitted that the Bill was clearly a piece of legislation which had been produced in a hurry when there was no real need for precipitate action. In the first place, he added, after the Bill was passed, the entire course of appeal would still be shrouded in mystery. At the time we had a Caribbean Full Court and a Magisterial Court. His comparatively short career at the local Bar had already made one thing clear to him. Even senior legal practitioners who wanted to prepare an appeal from one Court to another, might have to spend as much time looking up aspects of the law as Tom himself would have to spend in a month in ordinary practice.

The reason for this, Tom argued, was that at the time the only Rules providing for appeals from the Court of Appeal of Barbados to the British Caribbean Court were Rules which had been sanctioned by the Federal Court of the West Indies, the Federal Supreme Court. He suggested that some members of the House of Assembly would know from their own experience that the only persons who in fact knew the Rules were the President of the British Caribbean Court of Appeal, and the lawyers and the Registry of the territory from which the appeal originated. Other people would be unable to obtain the precise rules under which the Appeal was filed.

Tom had hoped that any Bill such as was then before the House would have done something to revise Appeal Rules and bring them up to date with the intention of consolidating the procedure as a whole and making it clear both to the public and legal practitioners how they could go about effecting appeals in different directions. The Bill before the House, it is true, did make provisions dealing with the transfer of the powers of the British Caribbean Court of Appeal to the new Court of Appeal in respect of appeals coming to the Court of Appeal. But it was totally silent, he regretted, in respect of appeals going past the Court of Appeal.[5]

3

Tom's contribution to the debates on the Bill was received with a silence that indicated respect and a measure of admiration. Honourable members on both sides of the House were impressed by the cogency of his argument and the authority with which he spoke. Young Adams was soon to show, however, that his knowledge of the Rules of the House could be used with such punctilio as to infuriate the Government of the day.

During his first year in the House, he took particular note of the way his father, then 69, was treated by the Prime Minister, Errol Barrow, and by some of his Party colleagues. Infuriated by the robust tactics being pursued by Sir Grantley, the Prime Minister said, addressing the Chairman of Committees: 'I want to tell the honourable member, who is Leader of the Opposition and a lawyer, that he should know better in the evening of his years than to come in here and try to destroy the country in which he was born. I say, know your place old man, know your place.'[6]

That was a challenge Sir Grantley was in no way disposed to ignore. Far from being a spent force, he had launched fierce assaults on the Barrow Government from the time he had returned to the House in 1966. The Prime Minister showed what was perhaps a trace of weakness when he said in the Assembly that he would not guarantee to be present in the House except on those days when he had to deal with External Affairs and financial matters.[7]

That was in May 1967 and his outburst in November of the same year may indicate that his patience with the Old Man may have been exhausted. Sir Grantley, still full of fight, replied to the charge made against him.

Rising to his feet the Old Man objected most strongly that he of all people in the island should be accused of doing anything to hurt the community. The worst thing he had ever done, he added, was to fight very hard to get the Honourable Prime Minister into the House of Assembly. That, he emphasised, was the worst thing he had ever done. For he had saddled the country with 'a tyrant, a dictator and a very abusive mental case.'[8]

The Prime Minister's reaction to these remarks can well be imagined. He objected to Sir Grantley's castigation, and the Chairman of Committees was requested to ask the honourable member to withdraw his remarks. Sir Grantley refused and a vain attempt was made by Ernest Mottley to calm the atmosphere by suggesting that both members be asked to withdraw the remarks that each of them had found offensive.

It was at this stage that Tom intervened in what had become a bitter and undignified wrangle. When the Chairman of Committees reported the matter to the Speaker, Tom at once pointed out that the motion to suspend Sir Grantley from the service of the House was not in order.

He took his stand on a Standing Order of the House, No. 36 (3). Basing his position on that article, he maintained that, when a member had persistently and wilfully obstructed the business of the House by abusing the Rules of that Chamber, then, if the offence had been committed in the House, the Speaker should forthwith put the question on a motion without allowing any amendment, adjournment or debate.

That was not the issue in this case because the alleged offence had not been committed in the House. Therefore, Tom concluded, with what seemed to be irresistible logic, that Sir Grantley could not be suspended 'from the service of the House' for the simple reason that he adduced. There seemed little doubt that the Speaker, Sir Theodore Brancker, was placed in an awkward situation.

Nor was this the end of the argument advanced by the Senior Member of St Thomas. If the offence, he continued, had been committed in Committee of the whole House, the Chairman should forthwith have suspended the proceedings of the Committee and reported the circumstances to the House. And the Speaker should then, on a motion being put, forthwith have put the question, 'no amendment, adjournment or debate being allowed as if the offence had been committed in the House itself'.

Tom proceeded to make his point as clear as daylight and one can well imagine the confusion of the Speaker and the growing irritation of the Prime Minister. But he considered it vital to clarify all the points that related to the validity of the motion. Moreover, he understood that the Chairman had never named Sir Grantley in Committee at all; and certainly he had no authority to name anyone in the House.

Irritated beyond measure, the Prime Minister accused him of filibustering. 'Filibuster or no filibuster,' Tom replied, 'we must abide by the Rules.' And, when the Speaker instructed the Clerk of the House to register his vote as against the motion, Tom replied spiritedly that 'No person (e.g. the Clerk) could cast a vote for the man that the electors of St Thomas have sent to the House as their Senior Member. Nobody could do that but that man. It had not been done in 700 years of Parliament — not in any Parliament conducted under the Westminster rules.' His colleagues in the House, among them Bernard St John, Burton Hinds and K.N.R. Husbands, supported him vigorously and the debate on the motion took up two meetings. In view of their numbers, their efforts were doomed to failure. In the end, Sir Grantley, along with Lionel Craig, was suspended from the services of the House for five sessions.[9]

After the suspension of Sir Grantley Adams and Lionel Craig, Tom Adams readily accepted the suggestion that their re-entry into the House of Assembly should be organised as a triumphal procession from the BLP's headquarters in Roebuck Street to the precincts of the Public Buildings, part of which was occupied by the House of Assembly. By all accounts, the procession was a conspicuous success, with Sir Grantley and Craig being cheered by hundreds of people who lined the route from Roebuck Street and Palmetto Square to the courtyard of the Public Buildings.

Though heartened by the unmistakable demonstration of sympathy, Tom could not help wondering whether the BLP was adopting the right strategy in its attempts to weaken the almost invincible support that Barrow enjoyed through the country. He seemed to think it was imperative to make a careful study of Barrow's character, his unquestionable ability, his methods of leadership and the secret of his success in establishing his popularity in Barbados.

While attending meetings of the House regularly and contributing in his own way to the deliberations of the Assembly, he appeared to the superficial observer to be keeping a low profile. Actually, there was another reason why he decided to play an unspectacular role in the House. He felt that within his own Party he knew of the jealousy and envy he could arouse among members because he was his father's son. And Sir Grantley himself was shrewd enough to recognise the folly of pushing his son too rapidly into the hierarchy of the Party.

5

Sir Grantley understood the situation facing his son as clearly as anyone else. When he retired from the Party Chairmanship, he himself made it plain that Party members were free to decide who would be his successor. It was thereupon proposed that St John take his place and the proposal was unanimously adopted by members. Before long, the Party had to decide who was to succeed St John as Vice-Chairman. There was a contest between L.B. Brathwaite and Tom for the vacant post and the former won by one vote. Tom was bitterly disappointed. Fortunately, Brathwaite and Tom enjoyed a good personal relationship and when Tom recovered from his disappointment, he realised that Brathwaite was elected Vice-Chairman because he was senior to him in the Party's hierarchy.

Tom persisted in the face of whatever internal difficulties faced him within the Party. For he believed that there were men in the group who would support him if he played his cards carefully. Moreover he knew only too well of the increasing support he was receiving from the Party's rank and file and he was therefore not without hope that in due course he would succeed in winning his way to the summit of power and influence.[10]

As the legislative term proceeded and began to draw near its end Tom realised, with agonising certitude, that there was a pressing need to organise the Party as a combat group that was capable of winning the next election. But he could not communicate to his comrades his anxieties and his sense of urgency. Some weeks before the election of 1971, he phoned me and said that the Party was in a bad way and he could not convince Bernard St John that defeat was staring them in the face. Would I try to see what I could do? My attempt to persuade St John that things were not going well was as futile as Tom's had been. He and other senior colleagues seemed to share a confidence that gave them a sense of security in spite of Tom's gloomy forebodings.

Less than two weeks before the election, Tom's political instincts gave him an even sharper warning. He came home one day and said to Genevieve; 'My God, I'm going to lose my seat.' He understood what was going on, rallied all his constituency resources, 'fought back like a tiger' and won.[11] Genevieve never admired her husband more than when she saw how he acted with vigour and determination to meet the crisis in his political life.[12]

In the 1971 election, however, Tom's Cassandra-like prophecy proved to be only too true. The BLP suffered a shattering defeat, and what made the defeat even harder to endure was the fact that the Party's Chairman, H. Bernard St John, lost his seat in Christ Church to a comparatively unknown political opponent.

Notes

1. Ronald Mapp, 'Master of Political Strategy', *Nation* newspaper, 15 March 1985.
2. Ibid.
3. Related to the author by the late Dick Walcott, 23 May 1986.
4. Ibid.
5. Hansard, House of Assembly debates, 15 Dec. 1966.
6. Hansard, 7 Nov. 1967.
7. Ibid., 6 May 1967.
8. Ibid., 7 Nov. 1967.
9. Ibid.
10. Clarence Jemmott to the author, 10 May 1987.
11. Letter from Genevieve Adams to the author, 19 April 1987.
12. Ibid.

SEVEN

Leader of the Opposition

1

One result of the electoral defeat of 1971 was that Bernard St John, who had assumed the mantle of leadership when Sir Grantley Adams resigned in October 1970, resigned the Chairmanship both of the BLP and of its Parliamentary group. Almost immediately, Tom was elected Chairman of both groups. From that time the majority of his colleagues and an increasing number of persons in the community began to perceive a new Tom Adams.[1]

He now set about making the BLP a far more effective organisation than it had ever been. He played a leading part in updating and revising its constitution, and he succeeded in modernising not only the Party's entire organisation but its constituency groups. It seemed clear that he felt it was his destiny to play the principal role in reviving the fortunes of the Party.

'It was then', wrote a contemporary, 'that his amazing capacity for hard work and for absorbing facts, statistics and information, however intricate or profound, was known. He soon caught the imagination of the public, especially in budgetary matters. He was the master of political strategy and missed no opening, however small it might have appeared, for a counter-attack'.[2]

No one was more aware of this than Prime Minister Errol Barrow. He had noted Tom's prowess in the House in the 1966–71 session of the House and realised that he would find in the new Leader of the Opposition a swordsman who was worthy of his steel. Indeed, so well aware was he of this that he made a serious tactical mistake during his 1972 Budget Speech when he spoke as follows:

The Rt Hon. E.W. Barrow: The Honourable Leader of the Opposition was given a whole week in order to prepare his Budget reply which I understand he had been doing in consultation with the Minister of Communications and Works (The Honourable F.G. Smith) because he even laid out the order of speakers with the Minister of Communications and Works.

Hon. F.G. Smith: Mr Deputy Speaker, I was out of the Chamber a moment ago, and I gather there was some reference to my preparing a budget speech in collaboration with the Leader of the Opposition. That is a damnable lie. ... I wish to make it quite clear it is a damnable and vicious lie, whoever said it, if it was said. I have not seen the Leader of the Opposition since the last meeting of the House, and, if it was said, it was a damned lie, it is defamatory and it is vicious and it could only spring from a perverted mind. (*Loud cheers*).[3]

The Prime Minister's reply that there was some mis-understanding on the matter and his attempt to reassure the Minister of Communications and Works that no offence was intended did not seem to be graciously accepted by the Minister.[4]

2

Barrow was convinced that the major factors which tended to impinge upon the Barbados economy would be found to lie in the international monetary system.[5] The pressure under which his Government was operating probably explains why the proposed salaries revision for civil servants and teachers was a source of considerable irritation to him.

He declared bluntly that there was some kind of superstition that the public service was automatically entitled to a three-yearly upward revision of salaries. That, he submitted, was the main preoccupation of the Civil Service Association which had recently dispensed with the term 'civil' and changed their names to the National Union of Public Workers. The latter, he contended, were demanding salaries for some public officers, higher than those paid to the Ministers of Government, and increases in pensions from 30 to 50 per cent without explaining how these increases could be justified.

He further charged that the leadership of the Secondary Teachers Union was militant and churlish and had staked their own claims on the earnings of the taxpayers, entrenched in the belief that they could hold the nation's children to ransom, blackmail the whole community and even overthrow the Government. He promised, however, that negotiations might take place if a sensible rather than the current insolent and truculent approach was adopted. He indicated the financial stringency under which the Government operated then; he declared that the appropriate time for increases would be the time when the country could afford them.[6]

This gave Tom the opportunity to launch a vigorous counter-attack. Why the constant attacks on civil servants and teachers year after year, he asked in seemingly perplexed innocence: Who are these militants? 'The only teacher', he added, 'I have ever seen on television speaking about Government or anything like that is a very gracious lady, the headmistress of

Queen's College, one of the most outstanding women of Barbados, the first female Barbados Scholar. Is it she who is being attacked as being churlish and militant? Is it not possible to hold a view in opposition to the Prime Minister without incurring his eternal and perpetual wrath? God help, Mr Speaker, the Minister of Communications and Works after today.'[7]

3

The truth is that the Prime Minister was faced with a difficult financial situation and Adams did not spare him the lash of his tongue. The year 1968 had seen a slackening of growth in the manufacturing sector. Decline in manufacturing output produced disappointing results in 1968 and 1969. Fluctuations in the level of sugar production caused inevitable problems. World inflation adversely affected Barbados' exports of goods and services.[8]

No one knew this better than Tom Adams but it did not deter him from launching a punitive attack on the Prime Minister. 'Now I am giving you fact from the horse's mouth,' he said, 'from the Economic Survey itself. The economy experienced no real growth in 1971. You will see that on the first page of the "Summary Information on the Performance of the Economy during 1971."'[9]

He continued, oblivious of the quality of mercy:

Mr Speaker, some years ago, Sir Alex Douglas-Home, the Prime Minister for a short time of Great Britain and now, I believe, the Foreign Secretary, described himself as a match-stick economist because he used to do his economics on match-sticks. We cannot quite call the Prime Minister a match-stick economist on this occasion. He deals in full boxes. We have to call this Budget the match-box Budget.[10]

A family group at 'Sunset', Tom's second home in Barbados.

With his father, Sir Grantley Adams, at the Bar.

Sworn in as Prime Minister by Acting Governor-General Sir William Douglas.

With Genevieve, being welcomed to the sixteenth anniversary celebrations of Nigeria, by Nigeria's High Commissioner to Barbados, and his wife.

At UN headquarters, Tom confers with Secretary-General Kurt Waldheim.

Ilaro Court, Tom's later home.

With Genevieve and their son Rawdon at the World Trade Center, Manhattan.

With the Queen and Commonwealth heads, June 1977.

With Canadian Premier Pierre Trudeau at the Commonwealth Conference, June 1977.

Left to right: Mrs F.A. Hoyos, Dr Elsie Payne, Genevieve, Governor-General Sir Deighton Ward, Lady Ward, and Tom at Tyrol Cot, May 1978.

Tom addressing the BLP Conference, 1978.

In spite of his efforts to organise the Barbados Labour Party and in spite of his performance in his first Budget reply, there were still some members who questioned Tom's right to the leadership of the Party.[11]

The matter was brought up at a meeting of the Party's National Executive Committee in July 1972. Fortunately, Lloyd Brathwaite, who had narrowly defeated Tom for the post of Vice-Chairman in 1970, was now firmly on Tom's side and introduced a vote of confidence in him as Chairman of the Party and Leader of the Opposition. The motion was carried after a lengthy discussion lasting until 2 a.m.[12]

The decision of the Party's NEC notwithstanding, there was still a lingering doubt in the minds of those who remembered his reluctance to enter the political arena before he actually did. Such members may still have been unconvinced of his commitment to politics and their doubt was increased when Tom at a crucial time decided to travel to the USA where he had been invited to visit American institutions and observe the American system of government. It was a gamble typical of a man who was as skilful at poker as he was to prove effective in politics.

In accordance with Tom's expressed wish, Lionel Craig, now one of his best friends, presented the budget reply.[13] Yet it seems that, as in the case of the WI Student Centre in London and his earlier efforts in the BLP, there were those who opposed his ascent to the summit mainly because he was his father's son and they disliked the idea of establishing an Adams dynasty.

Once again he was not blessed by the good fairies. Instead, he felt he was being pursued by a malignant fate that was resolved to demonstrate that he suffered from the disadvantage of living and working under the shadow of a great name. Tom, however, was determined to win his way to the summit of power not as a matter of succession, but by virtue of his proven leadership skills and ability.

When Tom Adams returned to Barbados, his absence at a critical time was discussed at a meeting of the National Executive Committee of the BLP.[14] It seemed as if some members intended to pass a vote of censure. The meeting lasted until 4 a.m. and the matter was fully discussed. At the end, the censure motion became a vote of confidence. Tom Adams showed, not for the first time, that he seldom, if ever, lost an argument. He was now recognised as the unquestioned leader of the Party.[15]

4

The 1973 Budget reply had proved quite incapable of coping with Errol Barrow's devastating rhetoric. And it was just as well for the Barbados Labour Party that Tom was recognised as the indisputable Leader of the Opposition. For without him the Party might have been almost completely demolished when the Prime Minister moved to amend the Constitution of Barbados in 1974.

The main issues involved in the amending Bill were the method of appointing judges, the directives from the Attorney-General to which the Director of Prosecutions would be subject, and the manner of appointing senior civil servants and members of the foreign service.

The Prime Minister at the outset stated his position quite clearly. 'My power base', he said, 'is the majority of the people, over fifty-one per cent of them, who voted for this party at election time. My power base is also secured on the collective responsibility of the Cabinet of this island, the unswerving dedication to the programme of the Party to which all the members on my side are committed not only today but on previous occasions, in times of engineered crises and in time of tranquillity.'[16]

A little later he added that he was not against persons and organisations expressing their opinions but he emphasised: 'we have been through all the democratic processes, through Cabinet, Executive, General Council and the support of the annual conference of our Party who are the masses who constitute the power base of this Government. If our annual conference therefore, representing fifty-one per cent of the people, who turned out to vote in 1971, and gave us the two-thirds majority which we now enjoy and which the people on the Opposition benches will have to put up with whether they like it or not, if they, the 51%, tell us that we have their approval, their consent and their support, we do not need anything more. ... '[17]

Errol Barrow spoke at great length and, to use his own words, made his position 'abundantly clear'. Unfortunately, he was angered by the widespread opposition in the community at large and the debate degenerated into personal attacks and provocative innuendoes. Had he been able to see into the future, his indignation would have been tempered by the fact that no attempt was later made by any subsequent government to rescind his amendments when they had the opportunity to do so. (More of this in a later chapter.)

As it was at the time his presentation was spoilt by what the Leader of the Opposition described as his 'brutality in argument.'[18]

Barrow said, in an obvious reference to Henry Forde, that he did not know any members of his party who had bought property next-door to a judge, an obvious reference to the Chief Justice, so that they could live close or opposite the residence of the head of the Judiciary. He said that he used to see the Member for Christ Church West (Henry Forde) at 6 o'clock in the morning jogging with the Chief Justice. He maintained that, if any member of his Party had been seen at any time with the Chief Justice in 'that kind of condition', it would be said that he was trying to influence the Chief Justice in decisions.

This at once provoked the Member for Christ Church West to intervene.

Mr Forde: On a point of order, Mr Speaker. If the honourable member is insinuating. . . .

Rt Hon. E.W. Barrow: I am not insinuating.

Mr Forde: Mr Speaker, I want the honourable member to make his position clear. If he is insinuating — he said he was going to hear who was influencing the judges — that I am influencing the judges, I challenge the honourable member to come outside of this House and repeat any such imputation and he would be sued for libel or slander.

Mr Speaker: No point of order.

Mr Forde: If he does not have the guts to. . . .

Mr Speaker: That is unparliamentary language also.[19]

Sensing that he might be getting under the skin of the honourable member, the Prime Minister continued as follows:

Rt Hon. E.W. Barrow: I am making a simple, bald statement that nearly every morning on my way to the beach I used to see the honourable member, before the elections in 1971, with the Chief Justice. I am merely stating that, although the Chief Justice and I were students long before he knew the honourable member, by the simple fact that I became Prime Minister, the Chief Justice has virtually stopped speaking to me so that he would not be accused by the other side of being influenced by the man who recommended him for the job. I am making a straight statement.[20]

Then in another attempt to provoke Forde's indignation he added:

> Is the member denying that I used to see him jogging with the Chief Justice, or that he bought a house opposite the Chief Justice? I am saying what would happen if any member of our party had done that — and I would not allow them to do it to be seen with any Judge.

Aware of the Prime Minister's tactic, Henry Forde wisely decided to hold his peace and control his rising anger.[21] Before long, however, tempers were to rise again.

The Prime Minister asserted that he had never been to the home of any of the judges. He had invited them to his home on Government occasions. No single member of the judiciary had ever invited him to his home consciously or unconsciously. He did not even know where Mr Justice Hanschell lived. He had never been to the home of Mr Justice Williams.

Then he sought to draw the fire of the Opposition by the statement that Mr Justice Ward was a member of the Barbados Labour Party, having not yet submitted his resignation from that Party. He declared that Deighton Ward was the only political person he knew sitting on the Bench at that time. Ward ran against him in the Federal elections in 1958 — he won and Barrow lost. Ward was President of a Trade Union. What is more, added the Prime Minister, 'since he became a Judge, sitting on a judicial matter when he had a procedural point before the Appellate Division of the High Court, and one of the barristers on the other side made a submission, Mr Justice Ward could not maintain himself.'[22]

At this point, Henry Forde intervened:

Mr Forde: On a point of order, Mr Speaker, Standing Order 28, Rule 9 states: 'The conduct of Her Majesty the Queen, Members of the Royal Family, His Excellency the Governor-General, Members of either House of Parliament, Judges, or the performance of judicial functions by any person may not be referred to except upon a substantive motion.'

Rt Hon. E.W. Barrow: If I commented on the. . . .

Mr Forde: To comment in this House on the conduct of a Judge in his capacity as a Judge is, I submit, contrary to standing Orders.

Mr Speaker: The honourable member has made a very valid point. The last sentence by the Honourable Prime Minister must be struck from the record, because it directly refers to one of Her Majesty's Judges in the performance of his judicial functions.[23]

The Prime Minister was not easily suppressed, however. After the Speaker's ruling, he continued:

That is alright with me, Sir. Before Mr Ward was appointed as a Judge he had the same misconception of a Judge's function, because on a political platform he said something which caused my solicitor to write him a letter.

This time it was Ernest Mottley who tried to suppress the irrepressible Prime Minister. He rose and referred the Speaker to Standing Order 28, Rule 10. But the Speaker, Neville Maxwell, a model of impartiality, ruled this time in the Prime Minister's favour. The latter had used the words 'Before Mr Ward was appointed a Judge'. That was quite proper, said the Speaker, for the Prime Minister was dealing with activities before Mr Ward became a Judge and when he was still in the political arena. 'That', ruled the Speaker, 'is not contravening the Standing Orders.'[24]

A lighthearted note was introduced into the proceedings by the Leader of the Opposition when the Prime Minister submitted that it could not be established three or four weeks before that Deighton Ward had resigned from the Barbados Labour Party. Adams made the seemingly facetious comment that Errol Barrow himself had not resigned from the Barbados Labour Party. The point need not be taken too seriously. For while the former based his comment on the fact that the BLP had received no letter from Barrow officially informing the Party of his resignation, the latter relied on his statement on the floor of the House and it was in the records of Hansard that he had indeed resigned from the Barbados Labour Party.[25]

5

Henry Forde started his main speech by saying that he had come into Parliament with the great expectation that perhaps for the first time in the history of this Parliament he would have heard a speech of great statesmanship from the Prime Minister and that he would have heard cogent and reassuring reasons why it was necessary at that time to introduce some of the changes which the Bill before the House sought to introduce. He added:

I am deeply saddened that at the end of a speech characterised by personal attacks, a speech characterised by a lack of clarity of thought, and a speech characterised by blusterings, political expediencies, the Prime Minister sat down and condemned himself in history's book as a man lacking in greatness.[26]

He had hoped that on the side of the Government there would have been someone left with a degree of independent judgement and a degree of objectivity to look at the nature of dissent in the country and to recognise the right of people to dissent and to dissent with some degree of bona fides.

He expressed the belief that, if these was anything which the present debate demonstrated, it was the conclusion that good men and women in the country must be cynical after hearing the Prime Minister's speech. For the latter's argument, submitted Forde, was that anybody who held a contrary view on the subject under discussion, no matter how sincerely held or how genuinely argued, was a complete nonentity. 'It is a great tragedy,' he added, 'that this little country of ours has not yet learnt to appreciate that not only one segment of the community, one political party, is interested in the progress of the country as a whole, but there are several others who feel equally strongly about the direction that we should take.'[27]

Forde then dealt with the whole question of constitutional changes and amendments. He commended to the House the comments made by the Wooding Commission in Trinidad on the difference between a democracy such as ours and a democracy such as Britain's with the Westminster model. He called attention to the forces which seemed to motivate or influence the amendments before the House and he dealt particularly with the reasons for the proposed constitutional changes. He believed, like Cicero, that governments of a number of men could be as tyrannical as the government of one; and he urged the House to look at all the conflicting forces in our society to see whether we could evolve a pattern of government which was more suited to our circumstances.[28]

Forde's speech was an attempt to raise the debate to a high level but no one who reads the long verbatim reports in Hansard will venture the opinion that his attempt was conspicuously successful. For, during most of the debate, the Prime Minister was an angry man, convinced that the widespread dissent in the island was 'engineered'[29] by interested parties. And of no one was he more suspicious of having mustered the forces against the constitutional changes than the Leader of the Opposition.

In stating his views on the proposed constitutional changes, Henry Forde made it clear that he never sought to attack people in their personal capacity, unless he himself was attacked. He emphasised that in the case of the Prime Minister's references to him, he would have treated his remarks with the contempt they deserved but for the fact that his assailant had the benefit of radio. He satisfied himself by saying that the Prime Minister's 'personal vindictiveness' towards him sometimes overrode his normal reason.

6

The Leader of the Opposition's attitude during the debate was quite different. He was prepared to meet fire with fire. In any battle of wits, he was confident he could cope with anyone and that included the fearsome Leader of the Government. The Prime Minister himself was not averse to engaging the Opposition Leader. But he was soon to discover that he was dealing with no mean opponent.

At the end of a long and somewhat involved sentence, Errol Barrow added the words 'no matter how depraved the Opposition Leader may be in his private life or in his ideas about politics .. '.

Adams rose immediately and said that what had started out as a harmless analogy had become a reference to the depravity of the Leader of the Opposition and he asked that it be withdrawn. The Speaker did not interpret the remark as referring to Adams but he asked the Prime Minister not to be 'so inflammatory' in his remarks in a general way. Barrow himself seemed to feel he had gone too far. He did not know about any depravity in Tom's private life and he agreed to withdraw the remark if there was 'any such connotation.'[30]

Adams was not in a mood to accept conditional apologies. 'The Prime Minister', he said, 'is in a position to know whether a man who practises the utmost depravity, whether public or private, upon becoming a Prime Minister and occupying that chair, then loses and ceases to practise depravity. I am not in such a position.'[31]

The Leader of the Opposition was not prepared to limit his bellicosity to that extent. He quoted from the *New York Times* which commented that 'A Scottish psychiatrist who had served as a consultant and practitioner at the Barbados Mental Hospital has observed that the high rate of insanity in Barbados is directly attributable to the frustrations of trying to become middle class in a hopelessly stagnant economy.'

Adams then vouchsafed the opinion that, instead of taking steps to remedy the economic distress and other obvious ills in the island, the Government thought it necessary to amend the constitution. The reason for this, and here he quoted again from the *New York Times*, was that 'the Government' — and it named the Prime Minister — 'walks a narrow line between rage and reaction and colonialism and subservience.'[32] On this Errol Barrow remained uncharacteristically silent.

Notes

1. Sir Ronald Mapp, *Nation* newspaper, 15 March 1985.
2. Ibid.
3. Hansard, 13 June 1972, p. 1054–5.
4. Ibid.
5. 1972 Budget Speech, Hansard, 16 June 1972, p. 1028.
6. Ibid., pp. 1031–2.
7. Ibid. pp. 1062–3.

8. Delisle Worrell (ed.), *The Economy of Barbados 1946−80* (Barbados, 1982) p. 4.
9. Ibid.
10. Hansard, 13 June 1972, p. 1065.
11. Clarence Jemmott to the author, 5 Aug. 1987.
12. Ibid.
13. Ronald Mapp to the author, 15 May 1987.
14. Minutes of the NEC of the BLP, June 1973.
15. David Simmons to the author, 2 March 1987.
16. Hansard, Aug. 1974, p. 3775.
17. Hansard, Aug. 1974, p. 3788.
18. Ibid. p. 3808.
19. Hansard, House of Assembly debates (Official Report), 27 Aug. 1974, p. 3794.
20. Ibid.
21. Ibid.
22. Ibid. pp. 3794−5.
23. Ibid. p. 3795.
24. Hansard, 27 Aug. 1974, pp. 3794−5.
25. Ibid.
26. Ibid., p. 3848.
27. Ibid.
28. Ibid., pp. 3848−52.
29. Ibid., p. 3785.
30. Ibid., p. 3791.
31. Ibid. p. 3807.
32. Ibid. p. 3806.

EIGHT

I Want to Make a Confession

1

Tom Adams realised that, while Henry Forde had effectively answered the accusations made against him in the House, there were many outside the Chamber who could not defend themselves and this gave him the opportunity to show how capable he was of dealing with so formidable an opponent as the Prime Minister of Barbados.

The Leader of the Opposition started by saying that the public of Barbados approached the fateful day of 27 August 1974 with some hope of a great and statesmanlike speech from the Prime Minister in which he would explain to an anxious public the reason why at this time of economic and other distress it was considered necessary to amend the Constitution rather than to take some steps to remedy the more obvious of the island's ills.[1]

Adams once again quoted from the article in the *New York Times* which referred to Barbados as 'no blasted Paradise now'. The author of that article wrote that 'the future of Barbados is very much in doubt. Independence from Britain in 1966 has brought disillusionment and even despair.'[2]

It was on this disillusionment and despair that

Adams hammered away. Who, he asked, after hearing the Prime Minister's speech, can be saved from a mood of disillusionment and despair? At the very outset of his speech the Prime Minister had given the assurance that it would not be an exercise in vilification, that he would not be attacking individuals.[3]

Yet the Leader of the Opposition was now forced to comment on the 'long, repetitive and tedious' speech that offered no real justification for the issues now before the House; and he deplored the attacks that had been made on a long list of individuals in greater or lesser degree. This included the Lord Bishop of Barbados, the Rt Rev. Drexel Gomez, Mr Clyde Brome, the Roman Catholic Bishop of Bridgetown and Kingstown, Anthony Dickson, Dean Harold Crichlow, the Moderator of the Methodist Church, the Rev. Philip Saunders, the lawyers of Barbados ('parasites and an incubus in the community'), Mr Justice Deighton Ward, later to become Governor-General of Barbados, the Chief Justice, Sir William Douglas, the Hon. Member for Christ Church (Mr Henry Forde), Senator H.B. St John, the Chamber of Commerce, the Barbados Youth Council, the Anglican Young People's Association, various Barbadian manufacturing and employers organisations and the Jaycees.

While upbraiding Barrow for his attacks on these persons and organisations, Adams reported, with little sorrow and certainly without indignation, the 'booing' the Prime Minister received in the Public Buildings yard not once but every time he appeared. Tom disclosed, with what looked like mock-relief, that the man who allegedly assaulted Barrow, pushing an afro comb in his face, did not come within 'danger distance' of the Prime Minister and was probably only trying to comb his hair.[4]

The Leader of the Opposition seemed to delight in pointing to some of the errors of fact that 'liberally littered' the speech of the Prime Minister. 'I am a sad and disillusioned man because I have made a mistake of thinking that the Prime Minister understood the Constitution of Barbados. He said he wrote it, he said he took it to London, he said he is very familiar with it, he said he is a constitutional lawyer and yet he says the Governor-General never writes me.'[5]

When Adams submitted that there was a component of agreement in the consultation process between the Prime Minister and the Leader of the Opposition, Barrow rose on a point of order and contradicted him, quoting from a booklet containing the records on the subject. Adams' reply was that whoever wrote the booklet was mistaken and it is significant that Barrow seemed to be reduced to silence. 'The fact is,' Adams said tauntingly, 'the Prime Minister has been caught out.' Tom continued:

He did not know, or he forgot, or he cannot understand it, or he did not write the Constitution. Nobody says that these appointments have to be agreed, but the question I posed in relation to the booklet is, is the Prime Minister going to deny that there is a component of agreement in the consultation process? The Prime Minister has sought to go around the bush in the course of which he has revealed that he does not know that the Governor-General asks the Leader of the Opposition if he concurs or agrees — maybe he does not realise that 'concurs' means the same as 'agrees' — in the Prime Minister's recommendation.[6]

Adams continued to use the rod of correction unsparingly. He expressed amazement that he was facing a Prime Minister of thirteen years' standing, who did not know a part of his basic Constitution and the functions relating to these important appointments. Once again Errol Barrow listened in silence.

———————— 3 ————————

During the course of the wideranging debate, the report of the Constitutional Conference of 1966 came under discussion. Tom Adams claimed that the report of that Conference was inaccurate when it stated that the Secretary of State, Mr Lee, had ruled, in the absence of agreement, that the provisions of the Draft Constitution for Independence were open to any Government *after independence.* At this point the Prime Minister intervened:

Rt Hon. E.W. Barrow: Mr Speaker, on a point of explanation, is the honourable member stating that what is printed in the report of the Constitutional Conference is incorrect?

Mr Speaker: The honourable member is not prepared to give way.

Rt Hon. E.W. Barrow: Is it incorrect?

Mr Speaker: Let the honourable member take his seat.

Mr Adams: On the evening Mr Lee said it was open to any Government *after election.* We in the Opposition delegations had good cause to remember that because we took that to mean that Mr Lee was saying that there would be an *election before* independence which in fact he was saying, but next morning when the Minutes came out, I don't know if the Prime Minister was there. Sir Hilary Poynton was in the Chair and when he read out the agreement of the day before, he read out these words that are here and pointed out it was open to any Government *after independence.* . . . We all know what happened.

We know about the attempted visit of Sir Lionel Luckhoo to Downing Street that night. We know he telephoned Mr Gerald Kaufman, the Press Secretary, and we know how this phrase *'after independence'* came to be put into the Minutes when the Secretary of State said *'after an election'*. That is something so indelibly printed on my mind as an example of how the Colonial Office does its work that I will never forget that as long as I live.[7]

Once again the Prime Minister was reduced to silence.

Later the Prime Minister referred to the fact that the ministerial system of government was introduced in Barbados without any referendum and without any discussion with the Jaycees or anybody else. That, he submitted, was a major constitutional change and there was no inter-party or intra-party conference. Even Party members were in the dark and they only learnt about it because the member for St Michael West (Mr Frank Walcott) was summoned urgently to London from Helsinki or Stockholm — he was not sure which part of Scandinavia — for the reason that Sir Grantley Adams wanted support for his adamant stand that the head of the Government under the new system must be designated Premier and not Chief Minister which latter title would make him seem like an African chief. That is how members of the Barbados Labour Party came to know about an important constitutional change. It was as a result of a by-product of an argument between Sir Grantley and somebody in the Colonial Office.

Adams at once rose on a point of order.

Mr Adams: Now, it so happens that I have recently seen, purely by chance, the private file of the gentleman in question which relates to these events. I have seen copies of letters sent by the Secretary of

State over the matter of Premier and Chief Minister, and I happen, just purely by chance, to be in a position to know the chronology of these events. It was in 1952 when he talks of the Stockholm arrangements. It was in 1954 when the status came in, and the incident went on for a long time. The Prime Minister is offering to show people documents, and I can show him some too.[8]

Rt Hon. E.W. Barrow: Mr Speaker, I do not profess to be perfect on that date. We had a system in 1954. If you have seen it in a document, I take your word that the document has not been changed. You say that the Secretary of State changed the document and the Report (re Independence) after we left (1966) and you have taken eight whole years to come and tell the people in Barbados what a wicked man the Secretary of State is, and I have been telling them that for a long time. I told Mr Lee at the Conference (1966) that he was a wicked man. Instead of corroborating me, when you knew that the document had been changed, you have waited until yesterday to come and tell us what took place.

Mr Adams: On a point of elucidation, Mr Speaker. It was the statement Mr Lee made that indicated there was going to be an election that caused the Prime Minister to tell him that he was wicked. ... It was the very thing that I said had been changed that gave rise to both of us saying that the Secretary of State was wicked. The Prime Minister because of what he said in the first place and the Opposition because of the fact that he changed it after.[9]

Thereupon the Prime Minister felt constrained to make an astonishing admission.

Rt Hon. E.W. Barrow: I want to make a confession right here and now, Sir. I can only win elections with the honourable member, but I cannot win anything else with him. He is too clever.[10]

Earlier in his speech Adams suggested that the demonstration in the yard of the Public Buildings had to be understood as symptomatic of the fact that the people of the island were fed up with the Government. In an aside, the Prime Minister muttered: 'Let us have an election then.' Adams at once took up the challenge.[11]

Mr Adams: Sir, I have heard the Prime Minister say in a *sotto voce* aside: 'Let us have an election.' Please, tomorrow dissolve the House. If you want to be challenged on that, let us have an election. You have said so in the House. If you believe you have public support, let us have an election. Every man in here has heard you.

Mr Speaker: Order: We will have no more strangers clapping in the Gallery.

Mr Adams: I have seldom had to accuse the Prime Minister of hypocrisy, and the rules of the House will prevent us from doing it now. If he is serious in all of the statements he has made in here that we have challenged him to repeat outside, that is my favourite. Let him go outside and tell the Governor-General, 'Let us have an election.' On this issue, or on any issue, I will try to promise not to mention the cost of living, unemployment, the crematorium, the harbour at Oistin, inflation and all of those things, but let us have an election if that is in the Prime Minister's mind really and truly.

Now, Mr Speaker, I have been diverted by words which are music to the Opposition. The Prime Minister was not a choirboy for nothing; he knows how to sing sweetly.[12]

After his admission of Tom's cleverness, Errol Barrow no longer appeared willing to accept the challenge to dissolve the House the following day and put the issues before the country in a general election. For the time being, however, he was victorious, with his Party using its two-thirds majority to pass the Barbados Constitution (Amendment) Act 1974.[13] But the significance of the protracted debate lay not so much in its passing in the House as in the two important results it produced. It consolidated Tom Adams' position as Leader of the BLP and made Barrow wonder whether, since he could not beat him in the House, he might ever win an election so long as Tom was alive.

4

It is not without significance that there was no Budget in 1975. The Budget speech the Prime Minister delivered on 30 July 1976, was the shortest such speech he had ever delivered and it was presented without a review of the economy. Tom Adams submitted that the last time they had received a financial statement was in the earlier part of 1974 and the people of Barbados deserved better than that. Moreover, the Leader of the Opposition was now required, in an unprecedented move, to reply on the same day that the Budgetary proposals were presented. Adams accepted the challenge without any feeling of trepidation and the Government may well have breathed a sigh of relief.

The truth seems to be that up to 1970 the economy had attained a measure of diversification, with sugar, tourism and manufacturing all proving important sources of employment and foreign exchange. 'Despite this,' as Dr Delisle Worrell has written, 'the first half of the decade of the 1970s recorded a poor output performance. Sugar production fell by a quarter and the industry was never again to regain its former position of dominance. At the same time, the growth of manufacturing and tourism slowed, as the period of rapid growth in the world economy came to an end. World inflation, stagnation of the main markets for Barbados' exports of goods and services, and rising transport costs caused an overall decline in real output in 1974 and 1975.'[14]

In the circumstances, it is not surprising that the Government seemed afraid to give the Leader of the Opposition too much time to answer the Budget Speech. Tom Adams seemed to enjoy what he regarded as a melodramatic situation. He pointed out, in an imperturbable manner that, while the Prime Minister had had more than two years to prepare his 1976 Budget, he himself was allowed exactly forty minutes to speak on so important an occasion. Strangely enough, there seemed to be an element of alacrity and joy when he accepted that challenge.

It appeared, he maintained, from all the statistics available to the Government and the Opposition that Barbados had made no real increase in the gross national product since 1971. In that year, he said,

the national debt of this country was $81 million. Since 1971 the cost of living has gone up doubly. Since the last election I believe that the exact figure is 124 per cent and, in an election year like this, if there was ever a time the people of Barbados deserved an economic review, deserved an assessment as to where we stand in the world, deserve an overlook, an oversight, of all the factors in our economy, it is this year of 1976, a year when all of us will have to face the electorate, and face the electorate with some words of our stewardship during the intervening period.[15]

Adams then proceeded smoothly from point to point, carefully concealing the time-bomb that he planned to explode in the Government's face as he drew near the end of reply. He touched on the question of tourism, claiming that the Government was as much to blame for its decline as were the economic conditions prevailing in Canada.

He pointed to the two by-elections, both of which had been fought on the primary issue of employment and both of which had been lost by the Government. Yet all the latter could do was make reassuring sounds, claiming that the unemployment rate was not as bad as the Opposition made out.

Then he proceeded with almost guileless innocence to deal with the question of banking. After a general survey of the island's banking system, he released his bomb. He charged that the Government had reduced that system to the ridiculous when on 30 May 1975 a bank called the Alleyne Mercantile Bank was licensed by the Minister of Finance with the initials E.W.B.

That bank, Adams asserted, was run by one Sydney Alleyne who had claimed, in certain sections of the New York press, that he would overthrow the political institutions of this island and establish a government of national reconstruction with the participation of the Prime Minister and certain members of the Opposition. Alleyne was described as 'a man of terrible disreputability', and Adams expressed horror that such a man was given a licence by the Prime Minister to operate a bank in Barbados.

––––––––––– 5 –––––––––––

But worse was to follow. Before the House and a wide radio and TV audience, he charged that certain members of the Democratic Labour Party had received from Sydney Alleyne such sums as $20 000, $5 000 and regular subventions of $600 a month before Sydney Alleyne's bank was established. Adams pledged to make photostat copies of the cancelled cheques and to make them documents of the House. 'If there is a Watergate,' he added, 'the Prime Minister will have to investigate that, not me.'[16]

Having shot his thunderbolt, the Leader of the Opposition then proceeded to discharge his last devastating castigation.

Oliver Cromwell once had to say in Parliament:'You have sat here long enough for any good which you might have done. In the name of God, go.' That is the one service which the Prime Minister has remaining to render to this Island after fifteen years. After today's feeble performance: after today's nonsense: after today's meaningless half hour, he has but one duty left to the people of Barbados and to the members of his Party, if any of them want to save seats. Call an election. ... That is the only thing left for this Government as bankrupt of ideas as it has admitted; it is bankrupt of revenue, and bankrupt of the capacity to govern this country. Thank you, Mr Speaker.[17]

During the period 1971–6 there was the complaint that a 'pretty total blackout' was imposed by the print and electronic media on the activities of the Barbados Labour Party.[18] In these circumstances, a less determined and less ambitious man than Tom Adams would have given up the task he had undertaken. Instead, he persisted in his efforts and began to feel he was forging ahead in spite of the difficulties that beset him. His oratory in the House frequently drew packed galleries of spectators and his eloquence on the public platform seemed to attract an increasing number of adherents. It was this that encouraged him to pursue his unrelenting campaign to reach the commanding heights of power and influence.

76

Notes

1. Hansard, 27 Aug. 1974, p. 3806.
2. Ibid.
3. Ibid.
4. Ibid., pp. 3831–2.
5. Ibid., p. 3833.
6. Ibid.
7. Ibid., p. 3817.
8. Ibid., p. 3905.
9. Ibid.
10. Ibid.
11. Ibid., p. 3833.
12. Ibid.
13. Ibid., p. 3967.
14. Delisle Worrell, *The Economy of Barbados, 1946–80* (Barbados, 1982) p. 4.
15. Hansard, 30 July 1976, p. 7079.
16. Ibid., pp. 7081–3.
17. Ibid., p. 7084.
18. Letter from Genevieve to the author, 19 April 1987.

NINE

Prime Minister

————— 1 —————

Tom Adams usually seemed unperturbed and composed in political and social life. Beneath that calm exterior, however, there lurked many of the anxieties of a hypersensitive mind. As the general election of 2 September 1976 approached, he would oscillate between confidence of victory and despondency of defeat. Sometimes, as he said to Genevieve,[1] he felt he was on the brink of a great victory; at other times he feared he would be crushed in defeat.

While he was still in London, Tom had noted the return of Errol Barrow to the House of Assembly and his meteoric rise to a position where he could promise to 'capture the commanding heights of the economy.' He saw him as an outstanding lawyer to whose all-round ability the Democratic Labour Party owed most, if not all of its force.

Tom could not help admiring the fighting qualities Barrow showed during the two years he spent in the political wilderness. At first, all was not well within the ranks of the Democratic Labour Party. In April 1958 F.G. Smith resigned from the Party and joined the Independents on the ground that it had long appeared to him that he had lost the confidence of his colleagues.[2]

However, fortune had already begun to smile on the DLP. Barrow saw an opportunity and was quick to seize it in order to change the political atmosphere in favour of his Party. That opportunity arose during a bitter industrial dispute in the island's sugar industry. That industry enjoyed a year of great prosperity in 1957, yielding a record crop of 204 000 tons. In addition, the price of sugar on the world free market had risen to a higher level than usual. In spite of the agreement that the Barbados Workers Union had with the Sugar Producers Federation, the former argued that the workers deserved an adequate share of the un-expected bonanza.[3]

Though many miles away, Tom Adams watched with interest how Errol Barrow handled the situation. 'In a historic mass meeting,' wrote Dr Richard Cheltenham, 'held on the second Saturday in April 1958, Mr Barrow, who emerged as a hero, made the staggering claim that the Sugar Producers had amassed in 1957 a profit of some nine and a half million dollars and could therefore meet the worker's demand.'[4]

The part played by Barrow in the sugar industry dispute made his victory in the by-election in St John later in 1958 a foregone conclusion.

There was another aspect of the situation that attracted the close attention of Tom Adams. He recognised the significance of the part played by Frank Walcott, General Secretary of the BWU, in Barrow's impressive victory at the polls. Hitherto, Walcott had publicly criticised the BLP on a number of issues. Now for the first time he appeared on the platform and threw the weight of the Union behind the DLP.[5] Tom, in faraway London, instinctively realised that this was to have significant consequences on the balance of power between the BLP and DLP.

Nor did he fail to be impressed by the manner in which Barrow went about his duties as a party leader on his return to the House. A Shadow Cabinet was formed in accordance with the practice of the British Parliament. Emphasis was placed on the need to have the Official Opposition represented in the Senate. It was cogently argued that the archaic system of double-member constituencies should be abolished and single-member constituencies established in their place.

With a Shadow Cabinet in operation, criticism of the Government increased sharply and before long the DLP began to see itself as a credible alternative to the BLP Government with more progressive ideas and improved fiscal policies.[6]

Tom was in no doubt that Errol Barrow's return to Parliament added dynamism and range to the DLP team. 'Nothing escaped their critical scrutiny,' wrote Dr Cheltenham, 'neither the Government's cautionary approach to public finance as reflected in a policy of budget balancing, or their policy to old age pensioners. On matters large and small they adopted a posture, and enunciated a policy. In a sense, they were all things to all men.'[7]

While the BLP, with Sir Grantley Adams attending to the exigent problems of the WI Federation, was in a state of indiscipline and disunity, the DLP, united and brilliantly led by Errol Barrow, went from strength to strength.

2

All of this, and the performances of the DLP, especially in the first two of its three terms in office, were very much in Tom Adams' mind when he was faced with one of the most crucial tests of his career. Could he in a general election defeat a man who had such a conspicuously successful track record?

It is true that the Barbados Labour Party had won

two by-elections in recent years against the Democratic Labour Party. In May 1969, the BLP, with Sir Grantley as Chairman, had won a by-election in the City, with Elliot Mottley as the successful candidate. In November 1970, it had won a by-election in St Joseph, with Bernard St John as Chairman, and Lindsay Bolden as the successful candidate. In both of these by-elections Tom had played an effective part. But hitherto he had been only a lieutenant. It was an entirely different situation now that he was in supreme command.

He knew he could cope with Errol Barrow in the House, formidable as the Prime Minister was in debate. But could he overcome the widespread loyalty and support that Barrow enjoyed in almost every part of the country? He did not claim the charisma of his father or of his principal opponent.[8] But were his debating powers in the House, added to his genius for organisation in the constituencies, sufficient to take him to the summit he so ardently desired? In the end he showed that his combined gifts possessed the magic power that brought him success.

His first trial of strength with the Democratic Labour Party was in a by-election in St Philip North in February 1976. That constituency was a stronghold of the ruling party and he could not help remembering that even his father was unable to win the favour of the St Philip electors many years previously.

Tom Adams need never have feared whether he enjoyed the blessing of the God of Politics. In the first place, he was fortunate to have as candidate a young man, David Simmons, whose friendship he had cultivated while he was a student in London. Simmons proved to be an energetic and imaginative candidate. He adopted the slogan 'No Tricks in '76' which, because of its success, was also used in the general election later the same year.

Simmons relied heavily on a humble but knowledgeable man, Ernest Johnson, familiarly known as Pabbo, but it was Adams who masterminded the whole campaign, determining what kind of speeches were to be made and in what area. He worked out calculations as to what support could be gained in districts such as Brereton, Ebenezer and Church Village. On the night of the count at Dodds, he sat next to the candidate with one hand on his shoulder and the other holding a calculator.

Even Errol Barrow was affected by the critical situation and came to Dodds with a considerable number of followers as a gesture to ensure that the voters of St Philip North remained faithful to a longstanding tradition. Both party leaders seemed to feel that the outcome of the by-election could have a significant influence on the course of politics in the island. In the end, Simmons won by 173 votes and Adams was so overcome with emotion that he embraced and kissed him.[9]

Three months later, the Barbados Labour Party led by Adams, won another by-election, this time in the City of Bridgetown. Here again he was fortunate to have an impressive candidate. She was a young woman, barely out of her twenties, Billie Miller, who at first seemed rather nervous and very reluctant to enter politics. Genevieve still has a happy memory of the day that was spent at their seaside house at Brighton when Tom finally persuaded her to try her luck in the approaching by-election.[10] Actually her father, Freddie Miller, a former representative of St George and Minister in the Grantley Adams Government, had given the assurance that there was really no need to worry about Billie. 'When my girlchild', he said, 'decides to go into politics, she will fight like a tigress to win a seat in Parliament.'[11]

Once Billie made up her mind, she proved how well her father knew her. She was not afraid to engage in battle and to take on anyone who was put up against her by her formidable opponents. She was successful and Adams thus won two by-elections in 1976. He was now prepared to challenge the combined forces of the ruling party.

3

In the general election later that year the Barbados Labour Party, led by Tom, scored a decisive victory over Errol Barrow and the Democratic Labour Party. He had proved that he could not only beat Barrow in the House but that he could defeat him in an election. Indeed, there was almost a complete turnabout in the political situation in Barbados. For, while the DLP had won 18 of the 24 seats in the House of Assembly in 1971, the BLP had now captured a majority of 17 seats.

The new government entered on an eventful and exciting period almost from the beginning. Before long it could claim it had expertly handled the Cubana crisis, defused the threat of invasion by Sydney Burnett Alleyne and his cohort of mercenaries, spearheaded Independence for Belize, urged pro-Marxist Grenada to hold democratic elections as it had promised, given aid to St Vincent at a critical time and re-established CARICOM ties.[12]

The destruction of the Cubana airliner and the death of all its passengers received the attention of the press in many parts of the world. The tragedy occurred shortly after the aeroplane left the Grantley Adams International Airport and as a result the first crucial decision had to be made by the new government.

The question immediately arose — why did the Government not see fit to apprehend the people suspected of placing bombs on the airliner? Why did it not seek to have those people extradited for trial in Barbados?

Tom Adams and his colleagues noted every aspect of the situation and decided to keep cool heads. And their caution proved to be the wisest course to follow. For, as it turned out, the Cubana disaster occurred just outside the jurisdiction of Barbados.

The circumstances that determined the new Government's decision were explained on every possible occasion. Perhaps no one made the situation clearer than Dr Don Blackman in a speech delivered in the Senate some time later.

The facts are that the aeroplane went down outside of Barbados' territorial waters which at that time was a distance of three nautical miles from the shore. . . . Subsequent to the Cubana airliner crash, new legislation was introduced which became effective on 1st January, 1979, to extend Barbados territorial waters from three miles to twelve miles offshore. This was done partly as a result of the Cubana airliner crash and partly it was done to establish uniformity with the provisions of the draft International Convention of the Law of the Sea.

During this time, intensive discussions were taking place within the United Nations for the development of the regime of the sea to ensure that its resources were exploited in a way which would bring equitable returns to all the countries. One of the provisions in the draft Convention of the Law of the Sea was that all countries that were not landlocked should extend their territorial waters to twelve miles offshore and to establish an exclusive economic zone, two hundred miles away from their shores, except in cases where the distance between several countries was less than two hundred miles, where a medium notional line would be drawn to give equal area to both countries.

The Government therefore had no jurisdiction to try or to seek the extradition for those persons suspected of planting a bomb on the Cubana airliner.[13]

The second source of excitement for the new government was the alleged attempt by Sydney Burnett Alleyne and a number of mercenaries to invade Barbados. That attempted invasion was reported by Interpol to the Prime Minister shortly after he had assumed office. Although Alleyne was not taken too seriously, the news that was flashed throughout the Caribbean generated a great deal of excitement. As a result of the general alert, the would-be invader was diverted from his supposed target and set his course for Martinique. There he was arrested on the charge of entering that island's territorial waters with a cargo of arms and ammunition. He was brought before the court, convicted of the charge and sentenced to eighteen months' imprisonment.

While Tom Adams took no chances about the threatened invasion, he seemed to enjoy the excitement that prevailed for a few days. Indeed, we were reliably informed that he loved the element of intrigue that pervaded the whole episode.[14]

Tom was by no means happy about the state of affairs he had inherited from the previous government. He called that inheritance 'an equation of financial disgrace'. He described the Democratic Labour Party as 'the lords of misrule' and emphasised that 'stern measures' would be required to save his administration from the financial problems they now had to face.[15]

He was at pains to point out that the new Government found the situation in the island's financial affairs very different from that which existed at the time when the Democratic Labour Party first captured 'the commanding heights of the economy' in 1961. At that time, though the latter claimed that the Treasury was empty, they were able to finance a crash programme for emergency employment for a few months. Moreover a deep-water harbour had just been completed and this, with the rebuilt airport, would give Barbados 'a launching pad for an economic take-off.'[16] In a statement in the House, Tom said:

At that time, the cost of living was rising by very little, only a few points annually, compared with a rise of almost 161 points, or more than 123 per cent in the four years 1972–1976. The actual record is 127 per cent in the last five years of DLP rule, 1971–1976, much more than any of our trading partners or associates. In many cases the rate of increase has been spectacularly more.

The strains occasioned by this failure to hold down the cost of living have had intense repercussions on the finances of the Government. The wage increases called for by the public sector in consequence of the fall of the purchasing power of their salaries were granted without any serious thought of reduction of wastage, and the former Government moved into the most unhealthy financial position where there was a regular and recurring deficit on its current account while of course it had to continue to borrow to fulfill a programme of capital works for the island.[17]

Adams had no intention at the time of giving credit to the former government for its level of achievement during its first two terms of office — for its successful efforts particularly in manufacturing and tourism, which became two leading sectors in the island's economy.[18] He preferred instead to dwell on the misfortunes of that government during its third term, though he did promise a full analysis of all the problems facing his administration. But he had no doubt that he and his colleagues were faced with 'a full-scale financial crisis'. In the meantime, he indicated in a brief outline what would be necessary to bring about 'a restoration of confidence in the management of the economy and an upturn in business conditions which we can reasonably hope will mean not only expansion in the private sector in the next few months but some relief to the public sector over the next financial year.'[19]

4

Before long, however, the new Prime Minister was to show that he would be guided by a broad, statesman-like view in leading Barbados to happier conditions, while pointing to the significance of its past achievements. That opportunity occurred when the island observed the fortieth anniversary of the revolt which started on the night of 26 July 1937, and spread from Bridgetown to the rural areas of the country. He described that uprising as a protest against the hardship and privation which the people endured during the 'hungry thirties' of the present century.

He considered it fitting that we should cherish the memory of those who died on that occasion, that we should remember the relatives of those who suffered and endured in the struggle for working-class liberation. Others whom he added to the honours list were Clement Payne and his principal lieutenants, Ulric Grant, Brian Alleyne, Menzies Chase, Mortie Skeete, Israel Lovell, Cephus Mahon and Vernon Jordan. Nor did he omit to mention W.A. Crawford, whose newspaper, the *Observer*, campaigned unceasingly to promote the cause of progress and reform.

Tom Adams described the uprising of July 1937 as 'a watershed in the history of Barbados'. He asserted that from that time a new trend in Barbadian affairs began, a new direction was given to the political, social and economic development of the island.

He noted, with an appropriate sense of history, that the social revolution of our times began with the career of Charles Duncan O'Neal, uncle of the former Prime Minister, and paid tribute to the man whose programme of reform was designed to change Barbados from 'a rigid, class-bound society to the healthy democratic state' it was to become.

He added that the revolt of 1937 gave rise to a powerful progressive movement and from that movement was born a political party and a trade union which worked together in close partnership and effected a far-reaching change in the character of Barbadian society. No one could question the greatness of the man who brought that movement to a high level of achievement in the political, social and economic life of Barbados. He meant, of course, his father. Nor did he fail to record the names of those who helped Grantley Adams to bring his labours to success in the early arduous years – Chrissy Brathwaite, J.A. Martineau, Edwy Talma, Herbert Seale, Hugh Springer, Gordon Cummins, M.E. Cox and Frank Walcott.[20]

Tom resolved to commemorate the 1937 uprising for a number of reasons. He believed that forty years before, there began a movement that was to effect 'a far-reaching change in the pattern of the Barbadian society.' He believed that all sections of the community appreciated the importance and significance of that movement. He held the view that the cause of progress and reform was vigorously promoted by the Barbados Progressive League, the Barbados Labour Party and the Barbados Workers Union and he readily admitted that it was advanced in due course and with no less conviction by the Democratic Labour Party.

Adams ended his Statement to the House of Assembly with words that indicated his abiding faith in the people of Barbados:

> Because we are serenely confident of the maturity of
> our people, because we are profoundly convinced of
> their wisdom and common sense, this Government
> has resolved that the day, when the poor and under-
> privileged rose in rebellion against intolerable living
> conditions, should be recognised as a Day of National
> Significance.[21]

The statement he made on 26 July 1977, provided no
little evidence that Tom Adams the political animal,
who asked for and gave no quarter, was well on his
way to becoming Tom Adams the statesman with wide
and liberal sympathies.

He attempted to strike the same note when he addressed the nation on the occasion of the eleventh
anniversary of the independence of Barbados. He spoke
with mixed feelings when he sent greetings to fellow-
Barbadians and well-wishers everywhere. For, while
he was pleased to observe another milestone in our
history, his pleasure was 'tempered' by the economic
realities the island had to face.

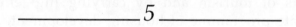

5

He pointed out that the celebration of the eleventh
year of independence was not the time for partisan
political conflict. The island's long-term interest must
not be sacrificed for the sake of short-term political
expediency. It was not usual to deliver national mess-
ages on a sombre note. But Adams emphasised, as he
had done from the beginning of his term, that there
was need for restraint in view of the difficulties facing
the island.

The plain truth is that no easy solutions are available
and I am happy to note that the great majority of

Barbadians appear to appreciate in a general way that economic restraint is necessary. ... This underlines the strength of a social democracy whose foundations were laid long before our time, later to be fortified at great personal sacrifice by some whom the older folk amongst us may still recall today.[22]

The Prime Minister was confident that Barbados would not follow the example of other countries where dissident groups adopted divisive tactics at a time of economic crisis. In this island even political opponents were restrained by the need to respect our tradition and to avoid spreading wild rumours and preaching ideologies that would undermine the stability of the country.

He assured his audience that their sacrifices would not be in vain. The Government had taken steps to expand our industrial base and already the number of jobs provided in the manufacturing sector had been increased by 855. He informed his listeners that efforts were being made to provide more work for the unemployed through the careful spending of funds by the Barbados Development Bank, by expanding the benefits of tourism and by carrying into effect an adequate programme of housing development.

If by setting ourselves the highest goals as a Government, we seem to be offering Barbadians a quality of life in the long run that is better than any enjoyed in the past, it is only because we place the highest value on the welfare of our fellow citizens and we trust that by our example others might be pursuaded to live and work, not only out of concern for themselves, but in the interest of their fellow-men.[23]

Adams by now had clearly demonstrated his mastery of the electronic media. His voice had the kind of timbre that captivated his audience, as a fellow parliamentarian was to say on another occasion, and to this were added a gift of modulation and a command of language that was given to no other member,[24] with the single exception perhaps of Henry Forde. There was no doubt that his experience at the BBC and his natural gifts enabled him to become a persuasive and compelling communicator.

6

The Prime Minister was also ably supported by the public relations campaign conducted by Henry Forde among Barbadian nationals living abroad. Forde informed his audiences that, when the BLP Government came into power, it inherited an economy which was staggering under the impact of the 1973 oil crisis.[25]

His Government, he claimed, immediately realised the need for draconian measures to arrest and reverse the trend towards economic ruin. Steps were taken, he explained, to reduce consumer spending, preserve the island's foreign exchange, initiate a policy of export promotion and pump new life into industrial activity. He quoted figures to demonstrate that these measures were highly effective.

He then concluded that recovery in the economy had been general, with all major sectors recording increases in productivity.[26] Forde placed special emphasis on the progress made by the Ministry of Education in implementing its programme for improving educational facilities. He pointed out that between 1976 and 1978 the construction of Community College, Roebuck Secondary School and the St Lucy Secondary School had been completed.

He also called attention to the massive programme of constructing primary schools that was being carried out with assistance from the World Bank. Ten new primary schools were being evenly spread over the rural and urban areas. New schools at St George, St Luke and St Patrick's were replacing the now outdated boys' and girls' schools which had stood for more than a hundred years. As a result the island's capital expenditure in 1980 would be twice that of two years before.[27]

In addition, the Ministry of Education had undertaken a programme aimed at providing secondary education for every Barbadian child. The St James Secondary School at Trents was completed with an eventual roll of 1200; while another secondary school at Wotton, Christ Church, also catering for 1200 children was planned for completion during the financial year 1981−2.[28]

The Ministry had also expanded and had given additional improved facilities to the old secondary schools − the Alleyne, Alexandra, Coleridge and Parry, Harrison College, Combermere, Foundation, the Lodge and St Michael's Schools; as well as to the newer secondary schools such as Parkinson and West St Joseph.[29]

Support for Forde's progress report on education was supported by an eminent educator, Mrs Enid Lynch, at that time a member of the Senate. It was her considered opinion that the development of educational facilities during Tom Adams' first term of government was the greatest such enterprise to be undertaken in the island since the days of William Hart Coleridge, the first Bishop of Barbados some 150 years ago.

In a speech during the consideration of the Estimates in the Senate in March 1981, Mrs Lynch declared that Barbados had reason to be satisfied with the general trends in education over the last five years. In addition to reviewing all the improvements that had been introduced during that period, she referred to a particular measure which indicated the spirit that animated the five-year-old administration.

We had that very bold step, which was a very bold step at the time, when the Minister of Education said 'by Monday morning I want all the fourteen-year-olds back into school'. It looked like a tremendous task, it looked a difficult thing to do, but it was done. We do not hear much about the results, but I kept in touch because I was associated with Dr Leonard Shorey, who was helping with the training of the first teachers for that scheme, and the children did respond.[30]

Senator Lynch's speech was of such a quality that it won high praise from the Leader of the Senate, Nigel Barrow. It was, he said, one of the most brilliant speeches on education he had ever heard, informed as it was with compassion, with wit, with balance and style and an impressive store of knowledge.[31] Tom Adams could have had no more loyal supporter than the lady Senator.

Another significant speech on the same occasion was that delivered in the Senate by Dr Don Blackman. The main purpose of that speech was to justify the Government's new constructive, progressive theory of social development as distinct from the old poor law administration with its 'welfarism', which, he submitted, had to be fought and destroyed root and branch.

When some people had to make fundamental shifts in thinking, he declared caustically, it could be a most uncomfortable operation. It had to be understood that there were serious philosophical differences in the process of educating such people to a new social development theory and this was something that caused 'travail' among them.

As a minister in the Tom Adams Government, Dr Blackman was responsible for all national assistance in Barbados. He emphasised that nothing could deviate him from his main purpose and that was to ensure that the rights of the people that his Ministry served — the poor, the oppressed, the dispossessed and the disinherited — were recognised.

What, for instance, he asked himself, was the purpose of the home help programme? The answer was that, in the new social development thrust, the home help programme was going to be devised in order to end the iniquitous practice of sending basically healthy people to live in the almshouse. It was designed to ensure that community care of a certain kind would keep these people in their own homes in which they could live out the rest of their lives in dignity and not be subjected to an institutional existence that was degrading, humiliating and disgraceful.

The Senator was pleased to report the progress made with the programme.

> We started off last year, with $100 000 which was voted for this programme. The success of the programme has been so outstanding that I was able to persuade my colleagues in the Cabinet. . . . substantially to increase this sum of money and this year we are now having, I am pleased to report, the allocation of $380 000 for the home help programme. Last year with our meagre budget we were able to extend this programme to ten parishes in Barbados, caring for 750 old people, and in the coming year we expect possibly to treble this in terms of the number of people that it reaches. We do not serve parishes; we serve people.[32]

It is fair to say that this and other parts of the Senator's speech were generally regarded as a tribute to the vision and the humanity of the Tom Adams government.

7

During the five years of their first term of office Adams and his Party worked hard to further the welfare of Barbados against the background of an international economy seriously affected by the consequences that followed from unprecedented increases in oil prices. He was ably assisted by the Great Combination, as his colleagues in Parliament were called. He was particularly grateful for the loyal support of his Deputy, Bernard St John, who showed no trace of bitterness over the circumstance that his 1971 electoral defeat had deprived him of the party leadership he once enjoyed.

There was no mistake about the success with which the island's economy had been managed. In the four years between 1976 and 1980, the level of unemployment had been halved, the level of investment had more than doubled and the Prime Minister was proud to record four consecutive years of real growth, attaining a record increase in real output of about 8 per cent. Moreover, nominal per capita income had almost doubled on the basis of almost US $3000 for every man, woman and child in Barbados.[33]

According to the Barbados Central Bank's annual report, published in 1981, Barbados experienced its fifth successive year of economic expansion during 1980. Sugar reached its highest level since 1971. Output in the manufacturing sector expanded faster than in the previous year and activity in construction remained at peak levels during 1980. And, in spite of a reduced number of tourist arrivals, earnings from tourism had still increased significantly.

In view of this sustained economic performance, the Prime Minister was pleased to indicate the benefits that all Barbadians had enjoyed as a result of the Government's remarkable achievement. A substantial reduction had been made in the incidence of direct taxation. And the value of this was further enhanced by substantial increases in wages and salaries throughout the public and private sectors.

The Prime Minister could not help showing how pleased he was with the record of his Government. Understandably, he ended his Budget Speech as follows:

> Forgive me therefore, Mr Speaker, if I am openly partisan at this delicate time in our parliamentary life and this happy anniversary in the life of our Party and end by saying, 'one good term deserves another.'[34]

Tom Adams deserved and was given another term. The number of constituencies in the island had recently been increased from 24 to 27. The Barbados Labour Party retained its 17 seats in the general election of 1981, with the other 10 going to the Democratic Labour Party.

During his five years as Prime Minister and Minister of Finance, his style of presentation and his skill in answering his critics won for his Budgets the admiration of friend and foe. And the success with which the Great Combination managed the economy made Barbados a shining light of hope to other countries in the Caribbean and beyond, who seemed to be floundering in a morass created by the international economic situation.

Notes

1. Genevieve to the author in New York, 22 October 1985.
2. Cheltenham, *The Political and Constitutional Development of Barbados, 1946–66* (Doctoral thesis, University of Manchester, 1970, published in Barbados by the Democratic Labour Party) p. 160.
3. Francis Mark, *History of the Barbados Workers Union* (Barbados, n.d.) pp. 157–9.
4. Cheltenham, op. cit. p. 162.
5. Ibid.

6. *The Democratic Labour Party: 1955—65* (Barbados, 1965) p. 18. Foreword by E.W. Barrow.
7. Cheltenham, op. cit. p. 182.
8. Hansard, Louis Tull, 18 March 1985, pp. 2074—8.
9. Simmons to the author, 28 Dec. 1986.
10. Letter from Genevieve Adams to the author, 19 April 1987.
11. Freddie Miller to the author shortly before the City by-election.
12. Aaron Truss, *A History of the Barbados Labour Party from 1951 to 1981* (Barbados, n.d.)
13. Hansard, Senate Debates, 25 March 1981, pp. 1680—81.
14. Letter from Genevieve Adams to the author, 19 April 1987.
15. *Barbados Advocate*, 25 October 1976.
16. Ibid.
17. Ibid.
18. Delisle Worrell, *The Economy of Barbados, 1946—80* (Barbados, 1982) pp. 3—4.
19. *Barbados Advocate* 25 October 1976.
20. Hansard, 26 July 1977, pp. 1517—18.
21. Ibid.
22. Radio and TV message by Tom Adams, 30 Nov. 1977.
23. Ibid.
24. Hansard, Billie Miller (City of Bridgetown), 18 March 1985, pp. 2090—91.
25. Notes for Minister Forde's speech on the achievements of various ministries 1976—1980, Nov. 1980, p. 1.
26. Ibid. pp. 1—2.
27. Ibid., p. 3.
28. Ibid.
29. Ibid.
30. Hansard, Senate Debates, 25 March 1981, p. 1650.
31. Ibid., p. 1688.
32. Hansard, Senate Debates, 25 March 1981, pp. 1682—6.
33. Hansard, Financial statement & Budgetary Proposals by P.M., 31 March 1981, pp. 5319—43.
34. Ibid., p. 5343.

TEN

The Pragmatist

1

After his electoral victories of 1976 and 1981, Tom Adams seldom if ever overlooked an opportunity to emphasise the need for political organisation. He would urge that special efforts should constantly be made to ensure that the programmes of the BLP were translated into effective action within a democratic framework and that they were so designed as to meet the reasonable hopes, expectations and aspirations of the people.

Those who sustained the Party during the years of opposition remembered the challenge he put before them. The electorate would never entrust them with the task of running a government unless they demonstrated they could run a party efficiently. To meet this challenge, the BLP was built up, constituency branch by constituency branch, study group by study group until its members were confident of being able to run a victorious campaign.

Adams was convinced that his party could not continue to win elections unless members concentrated on the minutiae of organisation. He emphasised in season and out of season that in no other way could they defeat the man who was still a charismatic figure. They had won the last two elections by providing platform speakers with notes on various areas of government and all the relevant material that was necessary to explain the Party's policy to the people of Barbados.

He also explained that the Party's command machinery was sufficiently well-oiled to take them through the 1976 campaign. They were happily free, he added with refreshing candour, from the petty squabbles and irritations that had marked every previous election in his experience.

In his address to the Party Conference in January 1978, Adams called attention to all this.[1] Moreover, he risked striking a discordant note when he said that they had fallen from that high standard of organisation. While they were going through the motions of internal activity, the continuous input of ideas into the day-to-day administration was being overlooked, if not forgotten.

Adams particularly insisted that the search for dynamic new political initiative must be a continuous one. Having won a heartening victory in 1976, they must not rest on their laurels but look forward to 1981, 1986, 1991 or whatever year the Prime Minister of the day chose to ring the bell. But they must not concern themselves exclusively with such things — vitally important though they were — as the Party's constitution, with its rules for constituency branches, standing orders of the National Executive Committee, procedure manuals for the conduct of public meetings and the conduct of elections with special reference to the method for the selection of candidates. All of this represented only the means to the end. The most important aim was to clarify to themselves and to the general public what was the philosophy of the Party.

This was imperative in view of what Adams described as the 'frantic ideological assault' that was being made on the island. That assault, as he saw it, was being launched by some UWI lecturers and a small Marxist Party which he was probably taking too seriously. He claimed, with some degree of exaggeration, that the people were being subjected to an 'intensive, indeed saturation level'[2] course of international Marxism.

——————— 2 ———————

Adams disliked playing the role of an anti-communist. He knew how unpopular such a role had been made by the notorious Senator MacCarthy as well as by the diminutive Hitlers and Mussolinis in some of the military regimes of Latin America. He knew, moreover, that Barbados was one of the few developing countries which had been able to make forward strides without proclaiming its adherence to communism or to anti-communism. Yet he felt that something had to be said about the doctrines that were being preached under the guise of 'scientific socialism.' The latter could not solve our balance of payments problem 'except by making people poorer so that they cannot buy foreign goods.' It ignored a basic advantage which had long been enjoyed by Barbadians — the principle and practice of free political elections. He charged that the chief expounder of 'scientific socialism' was a Marxist communist and he counselled the public against any ready acceptance of an alien ideology. In particular, he urged the Opposition not to sell its democratic soul for a foolish illusion; and added that the price a country had to pay when its political parties engaged in ideological war was already evident in the Caribbean.

A high point in the controversy over scientific socialism was reached when a non-Barbadian lecturer at the Cave Hill Campus, UWI applied for a renewal of his contract and was denied a work permit by the Government.

By way of contrast, Adams announced that the BLP had applied for full membership of the Socialist International, the worldwide Federation of Social Democratic Parties which at the time included the labour parties of Britain, Malta, Mauritius, Australia and New Zealand as well as the social democratic parties in Germany, France, Senegal and other countries which he found too numerous to mention.

It is significant that the BLP's application for membership of the Socialist International was supported by Adams' old friends in the British Labour Party and his application was readily accepted. Adams explained that, with its membership of the Socialist International, Barbados would remain firmly attached to the principles of social democracy. It would remain faithful to its responsibility for the social welfare and democratic freedom of the people. But he indicated that the Government would still be profoundly interested in the maintenance and development of a flourishing private economic sector in Barbados.[3] Thus he demonstrated that he was not bound by any narrow ideology but would seek, as a pragmatist, to promote whatever was in the best interest of all sections of the community. He told the Conference,

> What I can say with certainty, and what you, too, can be confident of is that before long. . . . Barbados will be well and truly launched upon a new era of lasting national development. We have already begun to lay the foundation and there are milestones along the path we have chosen which are clearly enough laid out to permit our members to shake off those defensive roles that I sometimes discern when we are attacked by those who misrepresent Government's policies.
>
> New building works and major highway improvements will in due course provide visible

evidence of these aspects of our programmes for development.

But in addition to these high visibility projects there are other initiatives of equally great importance to our nation.[4]

Adams complained that the 'fancy' expenditures instituted by his predecessors as the last election drew near were the 'crowning touch' to the severe financial difficulties left by them after their years of mismanagement. No government could be expected to be lavish with such finances as they had inherited in 1976. Yet he was proud to point to a list of things they had already achieved and to the plans which, when materialised at an early date, would be a 'living witness to the dynamism of the new regime.'

3

What were the achievements that he claimed? The five per cent Sales Tax was removed; fourteen-year-old pupils were sent back to school; more employment had been created in manufacturing and construction; the tourist trade had been expanded by twenty per cent; the Barbados Development Bank had issued more loans and created more jobs; the Transport Board had increased its fleet of buses, sending them into new areas and indeed into every parish; International Seafoods had guaranteed prices to fishermen and, as a result, the people were getting more food; Oistins was being re-developed and so was Speightstown; new polyclinics were being set up to look after the health of the people; more than twenty new industries were seeking approval to operate in Barbados; stricter control had been imposed on prices; tax relief had been provided for education and a $60 income tax credit for lower-income earners.

Nor did this complete the list of achievements and the plans that were being actively pursued. Employment incentives had been given to business enterprises; old age pensions had been increased and the number of pensioners had risen to 3100; the age of eligibility was lowered from 68 years to 65 years; the value of Government educational bursaries had been increased by 50 per cent; duty-free concessions had been given to agricultural and fishing equipment; an improved import-licensing system had reduced controversy and friction; an Export Promotion Agency had already proved valuable in view of the restrictions imposed on Guyana and Jamaica by CARICOM partners; the legal conditions under which women and children were employed had been improved; the subdivision of good agricultural land for speculative purposes had been ended; Bath plantation had returned to agricultural production; a department of Women's Affairs, a National Economic Council and a relocation of the Samuel Jackman Prescod Polytechnic were other achievements.

Tom Adams complained that one of the results of the fifteen years of Democratic Labour Party rule, during which certain political pressures were exerted, pressures which were increased by the Constitutional amendments of 1974, was to make members of the BLP distrustful of the concept that the Public Service could be impartial.

He considered it might be almost impossible to convey to the Public Service how resentful his Party members were about the political discrimination they had endured during the past fifteen years, about their exclusion from easy access to Government jobs and about the necessity to avoid subjects of political controversy when they finally achieved those jobs. He

mentioned all this not to be critical of the Public
Service of the past nor of the attitude of his Party
members but to appeal to all concerned to draw a
curtain over the unhappy past.

Adams knew that there would be difficulties in this
matter, but he preferred to take an optimistic view.

Speaking for myself, I have had every iota of cooperation and respect from the senior public officers
in the ministries under my control. ... It is time
that Party members appreciate that the Public Service
does not consist of a collection of saboteurs and
political obstructionists, but that the Government is
being given as good and sometimes better service as
any government in the past.

4

Having demonstrated the importance of an impartial
and at the same time loyal Public Service, Adams then
proceeded to make a significant statement.

In pursuance of efficiency and policies of localisation,
and in keeping with good social democratic principles, the Government has successfully established
a solid measure of participation in commercial enterprises. Through cordial negotiations, the Government has taken up or is taking substantial holdings
in the Barbados Telephone Company and the
Barbados Light and Power Company; has assumed
full management of International Seafoods Ltd; has
initiated a state-run commercial foothold in the
existing commercial banking system.

The Government's policy of participating in commercial enterprises is not confined to public utilities
or banks. The Government is prepared to seek out

and offer financial assistance to other local industries in vital economic spheres who may not even be aware of their own capital needs.[5]

The Prime Minister was careful to make it clear, however, that the Government had no intention of dominating such ventures but was quite prepared to finance their operations on development banking principles. The purpose of such assistance was to revive and improve the functioning of certain crafts and services which could be lost to the country if adequate funding was not made available.

Adams never indulged in high-sounding rhetoric but invariably aimed at measures that were practicable. He emphasised that such measures as he favoured were not based on reckless theoretical initiatives such as had thrown the economics of other countries into confusion and disarray. He always returned to the pragmatic position that his Government had a profound interest in the development of a prosperous private economic sector in Barbados.

In the address to his Party conference, he concluded:

I have spent a long time with exhortations and warnings. I have told you what I am against. Let me say a word in conclusion on what I am for and what our great Party represents. We stand for social democracy in the widest sense. We stand for the sort of open government that our record has so quickly and clearly demonstrated; for open discussion and deliberation, for decisions openly arrived at.

Above all, we put Barbados first, not ourselves; and I am confident that, when this conference is ended, the Barbados Labour Party will go forward with renewed strength and renewed dedication to the fulfillment of our destiny as rulers of our dear country in this difficult juncture of its affairs.[6]

Notes

1. Address to BLP Conference at Marine House, 29 January 1978.
2. Adams, 1978 Conference.
3. Ibid.
4. Ibid.
5. Ibid.
6. Ibid.

ELEVEN

Caribbean Man

1

From the early years of his first term of office, Tom Adams demonstrated beyond all doubt that he shared the convictions and aspirations of the Caribbean man.

When the Premier of St Kitts-Nevis died on 22 May 1978, Tom delivered a personal memoir on the man and the vision that sustained him. He was moved to do so because Robert Bradshaw was a patriot not only of St Kitts but of the West Indies and throughout his life he was fervently attached to the ideal of a united and self-governing West Indies.

He considered that Robert Bradshaw was an almost unique figure in modern West Indian history. Tom saw him as one of the leaders who had come to the forefront after the upheaval in the West Indies during the 1930s and placed him among such men as Norman Manley and Alexander Bustamante of Jamaica, Uriah Butler of Trinidad, Vere Cornwall Bird of Antigua and his own father, Grantley Adams of Barbados. What he specially remembered of Bradshaw was that he alone among the heroes who answered the call during the years of unrest, remained continuously in office and power until the time of his death.

Tom had known Bradshaw for more than thirty years and watched his influence spread beyond his native

land to other territories of the West Indies. He played
an active part in the Leeward Islands, rising to become
Deputy President of the Legislative Council of those
islands. He was inspired by the ideas of such doughty
federal spirits as Cipriani, Marryshow and Rawle. He
was the right sort of person to accompany Grantley
Adams when the latter went to London in 1949, on a
momentous occasion. There he joined with Tom's father
and others in the great enterprise of establishing the
International Confederation of Free Trade Unions.

Tom regarded it as significant that when the Federation of the Leeward Islands was dissolved in 1957,
Bradshaw joined with Grantley Adams in helping to
establish the Federation of the West Indies the following
year. He recalled that Sir Grantley regarded Bradshaw
as a trustworthy ally and made him his Minister of
Finance in the Federal Cabinet.[1]

Tom declared in a Statement to the House:

As long as I live, however, I shall always be grateful
to Robert Bradshaw for his loyalty and devotion to
my father. At a time of great doubt and uncertainty,
he was one of the men in whom my father was able
to place implicit trust and confidence. Five days
after Jamaica expressed its desire, through a referendum, to secede from the Federal union he
accompanied my father to London on a valiant but
forlorn effort to save the Federation from the tragedy
of dissolution. And when C.L.R. James proposed
that the Federal Labour Party should move in on the
Barbados election in 1961, Bradshaw responded to
the call with characteristic enthusiasm. Unfortunately,
the only other member of the Federal Labour Party
to follow his example was Joseph Bousquet of St
Lucia.[2]

2

Tom Adams undertook his first venture in the neighbouring islands when he answered a call for help from St Vincent's Prime Minister, Milton Cato. The latter requested help when a force of some forty persons took over a number of key points on Union Island. There was an urgent need to prevent the revolt from spreading to other islands of the Grenadines. Tom was convinced from his intelligence sources that the take-over of Union Island was but the beginning of a more general revolt in the Grenadines and on the mainland of St Vincent. He had no hesitation, therefore, in acceding to the request of Prime Minister Cato.

It was in the background of the capture of Union Island and the attempt on Palm Island that Adams resolved to take decisive action. The Governor-General and the Leader of the Opposition were informed, a Cabinet meeting was summoned immediately and the Barbados Defence Force was placed in readiness for action. The first detachment of the Force was sent to St Vincent and on their arrival a party of St Vincent police was flown to Palm Island.

The St Vincent policemen were able to land at certain points on Union Island but suffered a setback when they attempted to recapture the all-important airstrip. When soldiers of the Barbados Defence Force arrived at Arnos Vale Airport in St Vincent, they took over guard duty at Arnos Airport and this enabled a second contingent of St Vincent policemen to recapture the airstrip at Union Island. The various government buildings and installations were then recaptured and the revolt was effectively contained and then subdued.

In his report to the House, Tom Adams felt constrained to add that in the last twelve months there had been four insurgencies in the English-speaking Caribbean — in Anguilla, Grenada, Trinidad and St

Vincent. The attempted St Vincent coup was the only one that was put down summarily. That, in his opinion, made the lesson clear that, as in most coups, the first twenty-four hours were decisive. That, he stressed, clearly demonstrated that any policy of 'wait and see' was a policy of 'no assistance'.

He therefore commended the Government of St Vincent and the Grenadines for the resolute action they had taken and welcomed it as 'an assertion by a freely and democratically elected government that the forces of law and order will be used to ensure that the rule of 'one man, one gun' would not prevail throughout our region against the rule of 'one man, one vote'.

Tom was pleased to report to the House that the public would note that every CARICOM Government had supported the statement sponsored by his Government about the action taken by Barbados to prevent the so-called Movement for National Liberation from destroying all barriers against subversion in any part of the Eastern Caribbean.[3]

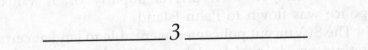

3

Tom's second venture in the Eastern Caribbean was more ambitious and more hazardous.

For some time he had noticed that certain forces had been examining the situation in that part of the Caribbean to see what could be done to develop radical political movements to promote the advantage of those powers in Eastern Europe which were planning their first positive steps in the western hemisphere outside their traditional sphere of influence in Cuba.

From the information he received he knew that many Cuban officers, who had been trained in intelligence schools in the Soviet Union, had been arriving in

Barbados, which was used as a central point from which these trained men went forth to Grenada, St Lucia, St Vincent, Antigua and St Kitts. These officers made contact with men who became household names in politics over the next few years; among them Unison Whiteman and Bernard Coard. Others were seen to be in contact with these Cubans from time to time.[4]

The Cuban movements began to spread, particularly in St Lucia and Grenada. Significantly, there were changes in government in both of these islands in 1979. In the first, the change took place peacefully; in the second, the government was changed by a coup which was not entirely bloodless, but was carried out by an opposition party.

'At the time of that coup in Grenada,' Adams later reported to the House in an appropriate Resolution, 'the Government of Barbados, in common with Governments in other parts of the Caribbean, was faced with a problem. It was a problem of a very special kind and character, that was not fully discussed at the time. Many of us were so glad to be rid of Sir Eric Gary and we were prepared to overlook the means by which his regime was ended. It was a classic case of looking at the end and ignoring the means.[5]

It is true that at a meeting in Barbados with representatives from Guyana and Jamaica, Henry Forde, the Attorney-General, and Tom Adams tried to give the Grenada situation an appearance of normality. They suggested that the Grenada Constitution or the powers of the Governor-General should be used to gloss over the uncomfortable truth that Maurice Bishop had overthrown a constitutional government by force. It was argued that Gary could be dismissed and Bishop appointed Prime Minister in his place but there was an understanding that an election would soon be held.

When it became apparent that the Grenada Constitution could not permit such a procedure, a promise was extracted from Bishop that an election would soon be held. Unfortunately, that promise was never kept.

Having read the captive archives of the New Jewel Movement of Grenada, Adams was able to give the House an illuminating review of the sinister developments that took place in the four-and-a-half years of the NJM Government. During that time we faced a revolutionary movement which was as fully ideological and as thoroughly committed to Marxism-Leninism as 'anybody in the historical academy in the University of Moscow'.[6]

The members of their Central Committee, Adams assured his fellow-parliamentarians, did not consider the plight of old-age pensioners. They did not discuss buses for the Transport Board, CARICOM trade and the two-tier exchange rate or the multilateral facility such as was done in Barbados. They were concerned about the commitment of the members of the NJM Government to the doctrines of Marxism-Leninism.

It soon became evident that Comrade Bishop was in serious trouble. The Central Committee used to give monthly ratings to all of its members. These ratings was given in ten areas and points were awarded from 1 to 5. One month Bishop was given 5 points for cooperation with the masses but only 2 for his commitment to Marxism-Leninism. On the other hand, those who gained most from the revolution were the faceless men who joined the Army and travelled abroad to receive ideological and military training in Russia or Cuba, 'the persons who were ideologues from their cradles practically.' These were the men who were dissatisfied with the progress of the revolution.[7]

The economic figures analysed by Adams showed little or no economic progress during the years of the NJM Government. There were no investments aimed at creating jobs, no factories or service projects to employ people. The only areas where work could be found was in government employment or in the steady growth of the Army. Yet an entirely different story was being told to the outside world. Adams said in the House that:

> The propaganda machine, fuelled, generated by dissident elements throughout the Eastern Caribbean, and indeed in the developed world, as well as the Third World, revealed Grenada as a paradise on earth compared to other West Indian territories. But the Minutes of the Central Committee reveal a constant complaint every week of alienation by the population, alienation by the inhabitants of Tivoli and St Andrew's, and by the women of St George's and different groups, and so everything was set, as we come into the year 1983, for an explosion.[8]

Things went steadily from bad to worse. The alienation of the people led to increased dissensions within the hierarchy. On the one hand, the ideologues wanted an increasingly hard line and on the other, Prime Minister Bishop was becoming more and more disillusioned. Perhaps he had begun to realise the weight of the arguments adduced by Edward Seaga of Jamaica, Eugenia Charles of Dominica, John Compton of St Lucia and Tom Adams of Barbados.

But it was now too late. He was told that he was to be Prime Minister in name only. The functions he would now perform would be merely to sign the decrees of the Central Committee and speak to the masses only as the occasion required. When he asked of what use he could be as the nominal Leader of the Government, his fate was sealed.

A little later he visited Eastern Europe where he tried to regain the good graces of the hardliners at home by singing the praises of Czechoslovakia and East Germany. It was to no avail, however. When he returned to Grenada, he was denounced in the classic communist style and placed under house-arrest.

4

Thanks to the British High Commission, Tom Adams was kept informed of what was happening in Grenada. He took counsel with his colleagues in the Government and members of the Security Forces. He learnt that others in Grenada had been imprisoned and held in Richmond Hill Prison in eight-by-eight cells and tied up for twenty-two hours a day. They were held in the condemned cell in the prison, as one of them, Lloyd Noel later revealed, and it was planned to start shooting them at an early date.

Tom and his advisers had to decide what they could do to save Bishop and those who were soon to be executed. Tom discovered from a reliable source that, if transportation was needed for any rescue mission, it might be obtained from a friendly nation like the United States. In the meantime he had already consulted some Heads of Government of the Eastern Caribbean. And he sought advice from the island's Security Forces as to what could be done to help the *de facto* Government of Grenada out of its deadly struggle.

The Barbados Cabinet met on that fatal day, Wednesday, 19 October 1983, and decided to seek help in mounting a rescue operation. But it was overtaken by the swift movement of events. On that same Wednesday, Bishop was 'rescued' from house-arrest by Whiteman, Radix and others of a large crowd. Instead of removing himself from the scene of activity, Bishop went into the centre of that scene.

Tom later received eyewitness accounts of the horrors that took place. There were armoured cars driving like latter-day juggernauts up the narrow streets leading to

Fort Rupert. These Russian monsters fired a hail of bullets and shells that killed so many people that they could not be counted. Bishop was captured, led into a courtyard of Fort Rupert and shot, along with Whiteman, Croft, Bain and others.[9]

Early in the day, following that tragic Wednesday, Tom called a meeting of the Cabinet to consider what should be done to meet the Grenada crisis. As a result of one decision, Dr 'Johnny' Cheltenham was sent to Jamaica to discover what Prime Minister Seaga thought about the matter. Seaga left a Cabinet meeting to speak to Cheltenham and gave the assurance that he would go along with a Caribbean initiative to deal with the situation.[10]

Later the same day, Tom spoke to John Compton, Eugenia Charles and others. Compton and Charles, like Seaga, considered that there should be a united Caribbean enterprise to meet the crisis. After these telephone calls, Tom called another Cabinet meeting which decided on a military intervention together with such friendly third countries as could assist with the logistic support necessary for such an enterprise.

In all of these proceedings, Tom Adams and his colleagues had to follow a very narrow path between secrecy and discussion on the one hand and frankness on the other. There was the delicate point that Adams had to be extremely careful not to disclose the secrets of one government to another.

On the Friday of that ghastly week, he made early contacts with the Organisation of Eastern Caribbean States (OECS) and this was followed by guarded phone talks with Prime Minister Seaga of Jamaica. Then he began a series of diplomatic consultations to which the diplomatic representative of Trinidad and Tobago was invited. Tom saw the latter with the ambassadors first and then spoke to him in the presence of Louis Tull, then Barbados Attorney-General and Minister of

Foreign Affairs. He was specifically informed that the OECS, along with Barbados and others, were seeking to attempt the restoration of law and order by a military intervention in Grenada.

Later the same day, Tom saw the Foreign Ministers of the OECS, who told him that their states had unanimously decided to participate in military action in Grenada. In the meantime, close attention was paid to Grenada itself. Emissaries were sent by Tom to the Governor-General of that island, Sir Paul Scoon, who was persuaded to give his approval to what the OECS intended to do, but indicated that he would issue a formal invitation when it was safe to do so.

For the remainder of that Friday, Adams made contacts with the diplomatic representatives of Britain, Canada and the USA. No reply was received from the British, and Canada was hesitant and indecisive. It was fortunate that President Reagan had visited Barbados and other Caribbean territories in 1982 and had become perhaps even more vividly aware than before of the strategic importance of the islands.

In the early hours of Saturday morning, the President was awakened and informed that an urgent request had been received from the six states of the OECS, Jamaica and Barbados asking the US to join with them in restoring order and democracy in Grenada.

Reagan at once gave a favourable response. He ordered units of the US Navy which were on their way to Beirut to turn south and make for the Caribbean. His reasons for this were twofold. Haunted by the nightmare of the Iran hostages, he was concerned about the safety of the one thousand US citizens in Grenada. Moreover, he was resolved to help restore democracy in Grenada and save it from becoming a 'Soviet-Cuban colony.'[11]

During Saturday and Sunday, staff planning in Barbados was well on its way between the Regional

Security Forces, the Jamaica Defence Force and the Barbados Defence Force. By that time Major-General Kris of the US Marines had arrived in Barbados. He and his staff were provided with an office, and joint planning continued. Those places in Grenada that were to be occupied by the Caribbean forces were identified. Other places were identified for assault by the US Air Force. To all these details, which were planned at the Grantley Adams International Airport, Tom paid the closest attention.[12] The operation, which was launched from Barbados, with the minimum delay, was successful, and there was no doubt of the enthusiasm of the crowds who welcomed the rescue mission with such slogans as 'America, we love you'.[13]

Perhaps no one was closer to Tom during the days before the military intervention in Grenada than Louis Tull. The latter considered that the Barbados Prime Minister was the finest orator the island had ever produced. Yet he was convinced during those critical days that Tom did not allow his eloquence to paralyse his faculty for action. Louis worked closely with Tom in the last 48 hours before the incursion into Grenada. As he said on another occasion in the House of Assembly, it was a period of high tension, of frayed nerves. It was a time when the Prime Minister and his Cabinet colleague were walking a tightrope; when, in fact, there was no time to rest and relax. Indeed, in the last 40 hours before they heard the voice of Colonel Barnes and Radio Free Grenada, announcing that the eagle had landed in Grenada, there was no sleep for Tom or Louis. They had to rely on the desks and floor of Government Headquarters to provide such comfort as was possible for their tired bodies.

It was during that period, as Tull said some time later, that, if he ever was in doubt, he saw at close quarters the strength of purpose, the strength of character and the capacity for decision of Tom Adams.[14]

Tom had every reason to be proud of the success of the enterprise. But he was acutely disappointed by the vote of the United Nations which condemned the intervention that had saved Grenada from a brutal tyranny. He derived some comfort, however, from the candid comments of the London *Times*. Of the 158 members of the United Nations, said that newspaper, less than fifty of them had governments that subscribed to the principles of parliamentary democracy and human rights.

Moreover, added *The Times*, the vast majority of members of the United Nations were dictatorships of one kind or another, but all of the kind which was ultimately symbolised only by the barrel of the gun and certainly not by the symbolism of the mace. Indeed, the newspaper declared caustically, if they saw a mace, most members of the United Nations would assume that it was not a symbol of the authority of the parliamentary tradition so much as one more blunt instrument with which to beat their peoples into submission and to pound words into a pabulum of falsehood.[15]

Whatever some countries of the outside world might say, Tom Adams was proud that the people of the Eastern Caribbean had shown that they had a love of freedom and democracy which had expressed itself in wanting freedom and democracy restored in Grenada. In the statement he made to the House, Adams said:

The Government has taken the decisions which we could not know were popular or unpopular at the time they were taken. We were heartened by the words of the Leader of the Opposition (Errol Barrow) who is unfortunately unable to be with us today.[16] We are heartened by the words of the Christian organisations of Barbados and of the people of

With President Carter in Washington, DC.

With Dr Eric Williams.

Gardening at his home in St George, 1979.

With President Kenneth Kaunda, August 1979.

Returning from Commonwealth Finance Ministers Conference in Malta.
(Genevieve is at the foot of the steps.)

Surrounded by Barbadian nationals during a meeting in London.

Election campaign, Bridgetown, Barbados, June 1981.

Taking the oath of allegiance for the second time; on the left, Governor-General Sir Deighton Ward.

With Mrs Margaret Thatcher.

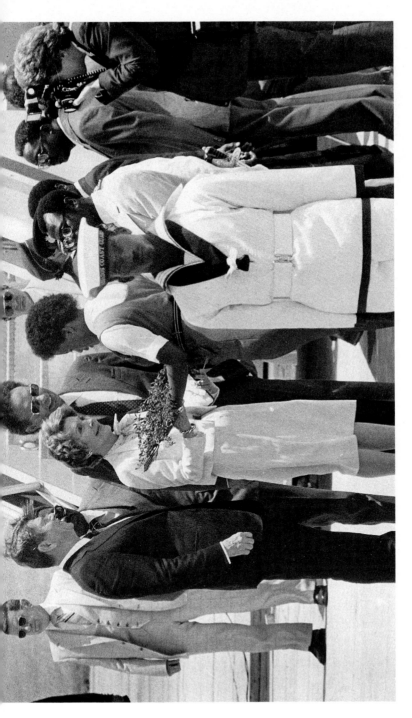

With President Reagan and Nancy Reagan.

Going out to bat in Barbados.

Barbados. I take this opportunity to thank the many hundreds of people in Barbados, the rest of the Caribbean and North America who have written to me and to whom I intend to reply personally. But it will all be in vain, Mr Deputy Speaker, if we show division or show lack of confidence in ourselves....

I am glad of the opportunity, Mr Deputy Speaker, to move this Resolution which stands in the name of the Government of which I have never more keenly felt the honour of leading than in the past few weeks of trial, tribulation and final triumph.[17]

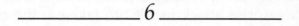

6

Erskine Sandiford added a felicitous touch when he spoke after the Prime Minister.

I rise as Acting Leader of the Opposition, to intervene in this debate to put the case for the Opposition and to state my own position on these very important matters.... I must start by saying that, generally speaking, the Right Honourable Prime Minister and Member for St Thomas has in his speech set out the facts, reciting the circumstances in a very statesmanlike and positive manner.... I must say his speech was free from personal invective and personal attacks and I think it is a tribute on this occasion.[18]

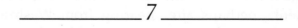

7

The Prime Minister was very grateful for the solid support he received in Barbados and other countries of the Caribbean. For it was not all plain sailing in the world beyond the region. A source of acute irritation to him was not so much the views expressed by a prominent academic on the Grenada issue but the refusal of a leading newspaper in the US to grant him the opportunity to reply to the criticisms of that academic. Arthur Schlesinger Jr, Albert Schweitzer Professor of Humanities in the City University of New York and a winner of Pulitzer Prizes in history and biography, published in the *Wall Street Journal* a strong attack on the decision to launch a rescue mission in Grenada.

He described US participation in that mission as a sneak attack on a pathetic island of 110 000 people, with no army, navy or air force. He quoted the words of Robert Kennedy when the joint chiefs of staff advocated a surprise attack in 1962 to take out the missile bases in Cuba. 'For 175 years', said Kennedy, 'we had not been that kind of a country. A sneak attack was not in our traditions . . . . Our heritage and our ideas would be repugnant to such a sneak military attack.'

Professor Schlesinger declared that the sneak attack on Grenada was undertaken without any effort to determine what the real situation in the island was or where the new regime was headed. While the The Times in London deplored the UN resolution condemning the military intervention in Grenada, Schlesinger applauded it, claiming that the action on the West Indian island had given rise to dismay and indignation throughout Latin America.

He then accused the Prime Minister of Barbados of being less than honest. He charged that Tom Adams had said at first that the idea of military intervention originated from a 'US official' and later withdrew that statement, 'perhaps after hearing from Washington.' He dismissed, almost contemptuously, the 'pretext' that the US had to intervene because six members of the Organisation of Eastern Caribbean States had asked the Americans to do so. His comment was that the US did not ordinarily form its foreign policy on the 'importunings of panicky states.'[19]

Tom Adams could not fail to accept the challenge to his integrity and to that of his colleagues in the Caribbean. In consultation with the Barbados Ambassador in Washington, Mr Peter Laurie, he drafted a reply aimed at publishing all the facts in regard to the Grenada tragedy and correcting the inaccuracies in Professor Schlesinger's letter.

First, it was categorically denied that Tom Adams made the statement attributed to him by the Professor, nor did he subsequently retract anything he said about Grenada. He and the Ambassador explained that the idea of rescuing Bishop, when he was under house arrest, and the decision to save Grenada from chaos after his murder were a sequence of events that escaped the notice of the Professor. They pointed out, patiently and not without charity, that Schlesinger was either unaware of, or chose to ignore, the traumatic impact of the assassination of Bishop and his colleagues on the Commonwealth Caribbean.

The reply submitted that Schlesinger gravely underestimated the dangerous situation that prevailed in Grenada when a group of fanatics murdered half of the government, shot a number of innocent men, women and children, imprisoned many leading citizens and placed the head of state under house arrest. Moreover, those fanatics had held the people of the island hostage at gunpoint by imposing a 96-hour shoot-on-sight curfew.[20]

The remarkable thing about the Schlesinger episode is that his letter was given prominence on the editorial page of the *Wall Street Journal*. On the other hand, the *Journal* refused to give Barbados an opportunity to defend herself and her Caribbean colleagues. It appeared to Tom Adams that this represented a breach of the basic principle of natural justice.

Tom's patience and forbearance were further tested by the positions taken by some countries at the Commonwealth Prime Ministers Conference in Delhi later in 1983. He and other Caribbean leaders, notably John Compton of St Lucia, had to use all their resources of eloquence and persistence to make their Commonwealth colleagues understand what had happened in Grenada and why it was necessary to take the action they did. Tom reported that the Conference was largely influenced by India, aided and abetted by the Soviet Union, and it was clear to him that the opposition to him and his colleagues was well orchestrated. He was, however, greatly encouraged by the Prime Minister of Australia, who privately assured the Barbadian leader that during the long discussions he suddenly realised that the Caribbean representatives were speaking with one voice and that the argument about sovereign states being invaded was completely irrelevant.[21]

In spite of all the vicissitudes Tom had to endure, he did not lose his capacity for relaxation. After the Delhi Conference, he and Genevieve, who had accompanied him to India, went on a vacation sailing up the Nile. It was something that Tom had always wanted to do and it was thoroughly enjoyed by both of them.[22]

Notes

1. Tom Adams to the author, 24 May 1978.
2. House of Assembly Debates, Hansard, 30 May 1978, pp. 886−7.
3. Hansard, Statement by Adams in the House of Assembly, 11 Dec. 1979, pp. 3166−9.
4. Hansard, 15 Nov. 1983, p. 50.
5. Ibid., pp. 50−51.
6. Ibid., p. 51.
7. Ibid.
8. Ibid., p. 52.
9. Ibid., pp. 52−3.
10. Cheltenham to the author, 26 May 1987.
11. Broadcast by Reagan over the Voice of America, 22 Oct. 1983.

12. Hansard, 15 Nov. 1983, p. 55.
13. Ibid.
14. Hansard, 18 March 1985, pp. 2074−8.
15. *The Times,* 7 Nov. 1983.
16. Barrow, in a radio interview with the press the day after Bishop's murder, expressed himself in favour of intervention in Grenada.
17. Hansard, 15 Nov. 1983, p. 57.
18. Ibid., p.58.
19. *Wall Street Journal,* 9 Nov. 1983.
20. Copy of the unpublished letter seen by the author during a visit to Washington during October 1985.
21. Letter from Genevieve to the author, 19 April 1987.
22. Ibid.

TWELVE

Vision and Reality

1

The telephone rang at Tyrol Cot on the morning of 28 August 1974. The caller was Edward Keith Walcott, asking to speak to Lady Adams. He congratulated her on the speech which her son had made in the House of Assembly the day before on the 1974 constitutional amendments. He spoke in glowing terms of the speech, saying that it was one of the best, if not the best ever made in the House. Even he could not have made a better speech, he added with the sardonic humour in which he sometimes indulged.

Keith Walcott's congratulations were of no little significance. As Attorney-General of Barbados he conducted Government affairs in the House of Assembly in the years before the Bushe Experiment introduced in 1946 a semi-ministerial system of government in the island. Under his forceful leadership, the House of Assembly came to be recognised as the most liberal in the recent history of Barbados.[1] He sometimes cajoled the House and at others coerced its Conservative majority to enact measures that provided for old age pensions, legalised trade unions and lowered the franchise. Much of this, it is true, was due to Colonial Office pressure and to the growing strength of progressive opinion in and out of the House. Yet it was Walcott who persuaded a sometimes recalcitrant Assembly to accept various measures of reform.

Under the Bushe Experiment, Grantley Adams became Premier of Barbados and Keith Walcott was stripped of the power he had enjoyed for years.[2] It was perhaps inevitable that an almost irreconcilable spirit of antagonism developed between the two men. As the years passed, however, Walcott mellowed and he came to accept the view that, while Adams fought him tooth and nail on a number of occasions, he always showed himself to be a man of principle.[3] When Grantley died, he expressed heartfelt sympathy with the sorrowing widow. Moreover, he had already begun to share the widespread appreciation of the ability of Grantley's son. Grace was therefore not taken completely by surprise when she received that telephone call from Keith Walcott the day after Tom's performance in the House.

2

Eleven years later, an even more enthusiastic appreciation of Tom's speech was expressed by Gladstone Holder, the spirited and controversial columnist of the *Nation* newspaper. Tom Adams was, in his view, 'one of the finest speakers in the world'. And on that memorable day of 27 August 1974, when, as Leader of the Opposition, he spoke against the constitutional amendments proposed by Errol Barrow, he made what was, for Holder, the finest speech of his career. Barrow had delivered immediately before, an oration which, in Holder's opinion, 'shocked' and 'shamed' Barbadians. Tom replied, without a note, in a speech that lasted more than two hours. As a result, Barbadians, Holder reported, were able to hold their heads up once again. 'He restored their despoiled dignity,' wrote the columnist. 'He was of course lucid and fluent and cool in spite of interruptions. He was also simple. Above all, however, his words were those of a man wise, dispassionate and far-sighted. That day he spoke as a philosopher-prince.'[4]

Gladstone Holder was particularly enthused by Tom's opposition to the proposals that related to the Public Service. The Leader of the Opposition (Adams) said on that occasion that the Prime Minister (Barrow) already had the right to be consulted before certain appointments were made to various posts in the Civil Service; and he also had the right to decide on certain transfers of persons who already held those appointments.

He added that in a small place like Barbados it could not possibly be denied that people who felt that a man with whom they were in daily contact, who had a right to decide on their future conditions of service, would demand more than their usual subservience to his political views and to his political prospects if they were to gain the promotions to which they aspired.[5]

Adams then warned that as soon as you politicised the Civil Service, as soon as you extended the area of political patronage, you were doing Barbados a grave disservice. All the proposed amendments to the Constitution led in the direction of more authoritarian government. And 'authoritarian' meant 'dictatorial' — it meant government by one man, government by authority, restricting the right of participation of people other than the ruling party.[6]

'To the bill in its present form we are inalienably opposed', concluded the Leader of the Opposition. 'I have spoken for a long time but I do not believe that history will find that I spoke to no avail. When the history of this particular Parliament comes to be written, it will be found that in the field of every victory, there is a great defeat. But those whom the Gods intend to destroy they first drive mad, and that is the only comment which I want to make to the final answer to the speech of the honourable member for St John who has just sat down.'[7]

There were many thoughtful persons who agreed with Gladstone Holder that Tom's speech on 27 August 1974 reflected the breadth and the depth, the clear-sightedness and the dignity of a philosopher-prince. 'It was a great speech', wrote Holder, 'delivered with punch and panache. It gave Barbadians hope for a new dawn. In recent years I have been moved to wonder where and why that vision was lost.'[8] And one of his greatest admirers, Senator Enid Lynch, though losing none of her admiration for the great man, agreed that Adams should have rescinded the constitutional amendments he had so brilliantly criticised. Had he done so, his Party would have maintained the moral initiative with which he took over the leadership of the country on 2 September 1976.

3

The fact remains that Tom Adams and the Great Combination never rescinded the constitutional amendments which their predecessors had passed into law in 1974. Had they done so, some of their supporters felt, they would have earned the appreciation and gratitude of posterity. This would have removed the weapon of political control over the Public Service and might have made its members more noticeably apolitical and comparable in some respects to the traditional model of the United Kingdom Civil Service.

There were three occasions when Tom Adams succeeded in breaking away from the spell of the 1974 amendments. The first was the case of Orville Durant, whose appointment as Commissioner of Police was allowed to go through without political interference. The second was Dr Keith Hunte whose appointment as Principal of the Cave Hill Campus, UWI, was made in spite of initial rumours of political obstruction. It is fortunate for Barbados that these two appointments proved to be conspicuous successes in their respective fields.

The third case did nothing to promote the cause of political non-interference. The appointee is alleged to have betrayed Tom's trust by using his position to bestow unmerited advantages to members of the Opposition Party. Adams was forced to take stern measures to counteract what was giving rise to widespread dissatisfaction within the ranks of the ruling party.

What caused even greater disaffection in Adam's party was the statement made more than once by Cameron (now Sir James) Tudor in his regular column in the *Nation*, that members of his own party, then in Opposition, received more jobs during the Adams administration than members of the ruling Barbados Labour Party. As if to confirm this, Adams was frequently accused of not doing enough to reward his party followers for political services rendered.[9]

Actually, as usually happens, in the ups and down of politics, there was cause neither for the ecstasy of satisfaction nor the nadir of gloomy disappointment.

After his victory in 1976, Tom approached the matter without the exhilaration of his more enthusiastic supporters. He pledged during the 1976 election that he would never seek to amend the Constitution of Barbados by unilateral action. A Commission for the Protection of the Constitution would be appointed on which all political parties represented in Parliament would be offered places.[10]

That Commission was appointed on 30 December 1977, under the Chairmanship of Sir Mencea Cox, with Ezra Alleyne as Deputy Chairman, to examine, study and enquire into the Constitution and other related laws and matters. The Commission reported on 29 March 1979, and the new Government proceeded to examine its recommendations.

Among the recommendations that were seriously considered were the following, some being accepted by the Legislature, others gaining the approval of Cabinet without reaching Parliament in time for acceptance:

1 That the Constitution should be repatriated.

2 That the Supreme Court should be empowered to decide on the constitutionality of legislation on application by *any* person, whether or not he had a relevant interest.

3 That there should be equal rights for men and women in the matter of acquiring citizenship, including citizenship by descent.

4 That certain words be inserted to improve the protection of fundamental rights and freedoms of the individual.

5 The monarchical system should be retained.

6 Any change in the form of government should be subject to submission first to the electorate at a general election.

7 The Senate should be retained and continue to have 21 nominated members.

8 Membership of the House should be increased from 24 to 30. The Government decided to increase the membership to 27.

9 That provision should be made in the Constitution for the electorate to be given the *right* to vote.

10   There should be freedom of formation of political parties.

11   That there should be an Independent Boundaries and Electoral Commission.

12   Control of Political Election Broadcasts should be the responsibility of the Boundaries and Electoral Commission.

13   Expansion of the functions of the Senate in relation to money measures.

14   Repeal of Section 79A so as to have the functions of the Director of Public Prosecutions completely free from control.

15   The nomenclature of Puisne Judge to be changed to 'Judge'.

16   The appointment of (Puisne) Judges should fall to the Judicial and Legal Service Commission.

17   That appointments to posts of chief or deputy chief professional or technical officer and of head or deputy head of a department should be made without consultation with the Prime Minister.

18   That there be consistency in the provisions for transfer of officers from the 'home' service to the 'foreign' service and vice versa.

19   An extended Legal Aid System should be introduced in lieu of the creation of an office of Ombudsman.[11] The Government, however, decided to create the office of Ombudsman.

These are some of the more than 100 recommendations that were submitted by the Cox Commission. Alas, the best-laid schemes o' mice an' men gang aft a-glay. Perhaps the most striking result of the 1974 constitutional amendments was that they were a major fact in bringing Tom Adams to the pinnacle of power in Barbados. Otherwise, it is difficult to understand their impact on the political situation of the day.

First, the DLP remained in office for only two years after the passing of those amendments. It is not easy to see how they could have done what they might have wanted to do in that short space of time.

Secondly, the BLP had little more than a year after the publication of the Cox Commission to effect any major changes in the Constitution. During that time a number of its recommendations were accepted and that, it is generally admitted, was due to the enthusiasm and the drive of Henry Forde, as Attorney-General. Moreover, when the BLP won the 1981 election it did not gain a two-thirds majority and would not have been able to rescind the 1974 amendments without the cooperation of the Opposition. Also, it was of no little importance that in the 1981-6 term, Henry Forde was no longer a member of the Adams Cabinet as Attorney-General.

If Tom Adams had succeeded in rescinding the constitutional amendments by winning a two-thirds majority in 1986, it would have been a great victory for his oratorical skill. And it could then have been said that the spirit of the philosopher-prince had risen triumphant over the exigencies of party politics. By that time, however, Adams was dead.

Notes

1. F.A. Hoyos, *Grantley Adams and the Social Revolution* (London, 1974) p. 100.
2. J.M. Hewitt, *Ten Years of Constitutional Development in Barbados* (Barbados, 1954) pp. 22–6.
3. E.K. Walcott to the author.
4. Gladstone Holder, *Weekend Nation*, 15 March 1985.
5. Hansard, 27, 1974, p. 3837.
6. Ibid., pp. 3839–40.
7. Ibid., p. 3842.
8. Holder, *Weekend Nation*, 15 March 1985.
9. Sir Ronald Mapp to the author on several occasions.
10. Barbados Labour Party Manifesto, 1976, p. 2.
11. Report of the Commission to review the Constitution, and to consider a system of national honours and a national table of precedence, pp. 175–82.

THIRTEEN

The Last Strenuous Years

1

In the meantime, Tom Adams continued to battle with the hazards of the prevailing international recession and at the same time to advance the cause of social welfare.

He made particular reference to one of his administration's achievements in 1980 — the vital piece of social legislation known as the Tenantry Freehold Purchase Act. By that Act, tenants, particularly plantation tenants, were enabled to own the land on which they were living. In other words, freehold tenure would be available to present tenants, and from this would flow several benefits. Tenants, who owned their land, could use that land as collateral to obtain credit. They could cultivate the land or build houses on it and they could leave it in their wills for their beneficiaries.

The new Act, moreover, would lead to a substantial development in the rural areas of the island. In conjunction with the Tenantries Development Act, Adams emphasised, it would ensure that complementary services of various kinds, such as roads and street lighting would be provided to enhance developments in the rural areas. These developments he regarded as essential features of the kind of social democracy to which he was firmly attached.[1]

In another direction too, Adams endeavoured with considerable success to inculcate the doctrines of social democracy. He urged the big business concerns to transform themselves into public companies and thus open the doors to wider ownership. And whenever he increased income tax exemptions he urged those who benefited from this to purchase shares in business houses that had become public companies as well as to buy Government bonds and participate in the financing of public enterprises. This he regarded as an important way along the road to economic democracy.

He was also keenly interested in cooperative societies where groups of people organised themselves to achieve a common end or purpose and to secure economic benefits. For this reason he exempted from income tax all the savings of Credit Unions. The flourishing condition of the Credit Unions today is a direct result of his active encouragement. It is one more example of the success with which he applied his principles of social democracy.

2

Thus he proceeded to deal with the problems of his second term. The island's foreign exchange position was seriously affected in 1982 by the deepening world economic recession. This led to a fall in real output, as had been the case in 1981. Tourist arrivals decreased sharply. Sugar exports showed no gains and there was only a modest growth in the exports of manufactured goods. Revenues in the public sector showed a very slow growth.

The Prime Minister, however, kept a firm hand on what appeared to be a gloomy situation. He succeeded in reducing its overall deficit by introducing strict controls on expenditure. By firm fiscal and monetary restraint, he managed to keep external payments in balance; and by borrowing from the International Monetary Fund he ensured an adequate level of foreign exchange liquidity.[2]

The year 1983 proved to be another disappointing year. Output remained at about the same level as in 1982, and most disappointingly unemployment rose to a high level. It was encouraging to note, however, that there was a rapid growth in exports of electronic components but there was no such happy development in regional markets for clothing, processed food and furniture made in Barbados. But the Prime Minister was able to bolster foreign reserves through foreign borrowing by public utilities, by government-guaranteed loans and by drawings under the Stand-by Arrangement of the International Monetary Fund. The most encouraging features of an exigent situation were that inflationary pressures eased owing to a levelling-off of import prices and an increase in local food production.[3]

3

By 1984, the things began to take a more favourable turn. The recovery in the world economy seemed likely to return Barbados to a path of positive growth and to give it a chance to rebuild the island's foreign exchange reserves. It was happily reported that, after these years of negative or zero growth, real Gross Domestic Product increased by 2.9 per cent. There was a remarkable increase in the exports of electronic components. Unfortunately, overall output of manufactures declined, owing both to sluggish local demand and to the contraction of regional markets. On the credit side, there was an increase in construction activity and a decrease in the rate of inflation. The chronic problem remained, however, in the continuing increase of unemployment.[4]

That same year Tom Adams had the opportunity

to show once again that he was still inspired by his absorbing passion for Caribbean cooperation and Caribbean unity. Some time had passed since the Fourth Meeting of the Conference of the Heads of Government of the Caribbean Community. He attended the Fifth Meeting, in the Bahamas, and expressed the hope that the reactivation of the Conference was a happy augury indicating that the factors which united the territories of the region were stronger than those that divided them.

Yet he was resolved to speak realistically on the situation that faced the region. He urged that the Conference should undertake its deliberations with a sense of urgency and seriousness. CARICOM and the Caribbean were, he submitted, more important than ever to West Indians for a number of political and economic reasons.

He did not attempt to conceal the melancholy fact that since the Fourth Conference, which had been held in Trinidad, the regional integration movement had sustained what could only be described as a hammering. He referred to the economic difficulties and barriers which had been identified during the fourth Conference. Hardly any of these, he regretted, had been overcome; some had worsened; and all this in spite of the successful acquisition of funds for financing LIAT and WISCO.

It was tragic that in these circumstances CARICOM had not benefited sufficiently from the economic turnaround in some major industrial countries such as the USA. Instead, certain sectors of the West Indian economy — petroleum, bauxite and citrus — had continued to decline. To make matters worse, CARICOM countries, in the depressed state of their economies, were adopting a policy of protectionism more and more. Therein lay the tragedy of our situation, with the disastrous tendency for economic slump and trade protection to feed on each other. No wonder the growth of trade was stunted, with protectionist trade increasingly eating away at the heart of the Common Market.

Tom Adams was in no mood to mince his words. 'There have been accusations of cheating as efforts have been made to circumvent the Rules of Origin,' he told the Conference:

> Exchange rates have become increasingly divergent. The CARICOM Multilateral Clearing Facility (CMCF) still founders; the promises, indeed decisions of Port-of-Spain .... are yet unfulfilled. Partly because of protectionism in the industrialised world, it has become increasingly difficult to penetrate overseas markets. The entire trade regime in CARICOM has deteriorated further since the Fourth Conference. The upshot is that the harmonisation of economic policy, the *raison d'être* of our economic union and Community, is in disarray.[5]

But Adams was no cynic, content to say that CARICOM was being reduced to an economic community without an economic policy. He was not the sort of pessimist to make the gloomy prophecy that the CARICOM territories, though in different stages of distress, were likely to miss the benefits of the recovery which the industrialised countries were now experiencing.

Instead, he urged the Conference to give careful study to the paper which they had commissioned on the subject of 'structural adjustment'. He described that paper as candid and clear both in its arguments and its recommendations. It would do nothing to relieve our parlous economic situation if we were merely to note its contents and then place it in a bureaucratic pigeon-hole. He added:

> The aim of this Conference must be to agree on measures that will maintain the spirit of unity, and

to remember that success is best achieved in a political climate of freedom, liberty and security. In such a climate, the spirit of compromise can thrive.

Barbados comes to this Conference in a spirit of compromise. We shall seek to avoid fighting yesterday's battles today and we shall do our best to avoid raking over the ashes of the past. I am minded, Sir, that we may not always get on well together but we need each other. Providence in the shape of geography, history and culture has thrown us together and we must show that we have been thrown together for better, not worse.[6]

It is one of the tragedies of West Indian history that this was the last Conference of this kind that Tom Adams was to attend.

4

In Barbados Adams continued to work with unstinting energy to benefit from the recovery of the world economy. He was resolved that when the time was opportune the island should be able to derive the greatest advantage possible from the economic recovery of the world's industrialised countries.

In January 1984, he opened Heywoods Hotel and the Speightstown By-pass. He described the hotel as an addition of a special quality to the tourist facilities in the island. It was located in the north because it reflected two aspects of his Government's policy. First, there was an abundance of tourist accommodation and activity on the south and west coasts and it would be advantageous for the whole country if further development took place in the northern and eastern areas of Barbados.

Another point of significance made by the Prime Minister was that Heywoods and the Speightstown

Pass was only part of the development of the northern section of the island. Speightstown, he promised, would be allowed to recapture some of the glory it once enjoyed. Bridgetown and the St Michael and central areas would be maintained in their traditional momentum; the outer parishes would be developed; and Oistins would continue to be the focus of development in the south. But Speightstown would again recapture some of the glory of its recent past.

Other elements for the development plan for the north were also mentioned. There had already been the Spring Hall Land Lease project in St Lucy, the factory complex at Six Men's and the Polyclinic at Litchfield which had been in operation for some years. Above all, there was the Cement Plant at Checker Hall, described by Adams as the largest industrial project in the Eastern Caribbean. Moreover, the roads between the Cement Plant and its shale quarry at Greenland, St Andrew, were to be reconstructed as part of the Government's major highway development.[7]

In addition to these and other projects, there was Tom Adams' great dream. That was to build a major highway from the Deep Water Harbour and the Grantley Adams International Airport. The vision entertained by the Prime Minister was that this would provide the major portion of the infrastructure that would make Barbados the great industrial centre of the Caribbean.

By April 1984 Adams began to show signs of the strain imposed by his labours during the past three years. When he delivered his Budget speech on 17 April he made some remarks that some may have regarded as a portent.

It is not usual in Budgetary presentations to touch on a personal note; but on this occasion I feel constrained to depart from the norm and say that never before have I felt so great a sense of pressure leading

138

up to my financial proposals as this year. For the last three years, certain defensive skills have been required of Barbados' Minister of Finance....

With the support of all sectors of our community we have held that strain and kept our heads above water. With the continued strength of the international economic recovery we are now poised to start swimming again.[8]

Three months later he was faced with a challenge he could not ignore. It was a by-election in St Peter in July, caused by the resignation, owing to illness, of Burton Hinds, a BLP member and Speaker of the House. When the votes were counted, Sybil Leacock, a DLP member, won by one vote, defeating Owen Arthur, the BLP member.

Adams appealed to the Courts, alleging an electoral irregularity and his appeal was upheld. The by-election was held again, this time in November. In July he had left the campaign largely to BLP officials. This time he moved into St Peter and took up residence in the parish. He assumed personal command of the campaign and his energetic house-to-house campaign and his platform eloquence ensured victory for Owen Arthur by a convincing majority.

By this time Adams could not conceal from himself the strain he was undergoing. Later in 1984 his friend, Dr Bertie Clarke, referred him to a cardiologist, Dr Richard Sutton, at 149 Harley Street, London. The specialist sent a full report to Dr Trevor Hassell.[9] Tom told his wife, on his return to Barbados, that his condition was diagnosed as due to a cardiac source and that open-heart surgery was recommended.[10]

Genevieve herself had for some time suspected the cause of his trouble. For when she put her hand on his chest, she could feel the irregular thumping of his heart. She knew also that he had told his son Douglas that at times he was so tired he did not know how long he would be able to carry on.[11]

Genevieve had come to realise for some time that Tom was 'a prime heart-attack person'. Besides the irregularity of his heartbeat he was now 53 years old and overweight, drank rather too much on convivial occasions, ate too much of the wrong foods, took no exercise whatever after giving up work in his garden, and held one of the most stressful jobs in the island. He rarely slept more than four hours a day and worked hard and played hard.[12] Looking back, Genevieve could say that it was a wonder he did not collapse sooner.

Yet Adams paid no immediate attention to the advice of the Harley Street specialist. He had obtained the necessary loan to build the great highway of his dream — from the Deep Water Harbour to the Grantley Adams International Airport. Now, early in 1985, he set out to Japan to seek a loan to further and complete the plans of his Government.

In February he passed through New York on his way to Tokyo. His mission was successful and he signed the agreement guaranteeing the loan. On his way back, he had dinner in New York with the Barbados Consul General, Randolph Field, whom he informed, almost casually, of his heart condition. After over-nighting in New York and before returning to Barbados, he stopped in at Jamaica where the CARICOM Heads of Government met Brian Mulrony, the recently-elected Prime Minister of Canada. All of that was in February 1985.

Genevieve did not accompany Tom on any of these trips, but he called her from Japan and from New York and Jamaica. He also brought her back from Japan a superb camera which is still one of her cherished possessions. One of the gifts he gave her on his return was a perfume called 'Forget Me Not'.[13]

5

In spite of the advice he had received from the London specialist, Adams did not let up in his activities.

Friday evening, 8 March, promised to be an exciting occasion. A meeting had been called in St Albans Junior School to announce that Lionel Craig was transferring his allegiance from St James North to St Michael South, a constituency held by the redoubtable Erskine Sandiford of the DLP. It had been reported that Adams was to address the meeting and it was to this that the people were looking forward. The atmosphere was one of excitement and expectation.

When Adams arrived it was clear that he was in a fighting mood. There was no doubt that he was already working on a master plan for the general election that was constitutionally due in 1986. The crowd, that cheered him to the echo, were exhorted to bear in mind that the name of the game was winning.

When he finished speaking, the crowd sang 'For he's a Jolly Good Fellow' and Adams, raising his hands high above his head, sang as lustily as anyone else.[14] No one knew that this was his last speech and that on the Monday following he was destined to die from cardiac failure.

The last few days that Tom and Genevieve spent together were quiet and very peaceful. It seemed to 'Gen', as he used to call her, that Tom was very, very tired but otherwise everything was OK. They walked together in the gardens and they talked about this and that while Tom shaved with an electric razor. To her pleasant surprise, Tom donned a bathing suit and bathed in the pool as if he was seeking some release from the tensions that were consuming him. Then they listened to music and watched videos for the rest of that Saturday morning and early afternoon.[15] He told Genevieve he did not feel like going to the races.

But she realised he would have to attend because the Gold Cup contest made it a special event.[16]

At the races, he spoke for a few minutes with a young lady who used to say that, when she saw Tom on television, his voice, his eloquence and his diction made her feel proud of her Prime Minister. To her he seemed to be his usual elegant and charming self.[17] Then he moved around talking to others, whether friends or opponents, as if he had no care in the world. That evening he spent quietly at Ilaro Court.

On Sunday he again lingered at Ilaro Court as if he was unwilling to go beyond its precincts. He spent most of the day at home until the early evening when he visited his constituents in St Thomas. The President of the St Thomas Constituency Branch of the BLP, Miss Cynthia Forde, reported that plans were considered for the forthcoming St Thomas Festival and the meeting that evening was 'the usual jovial one'. But she said later that 'the thing I remember distinctly about last Sunday's meeting, March 10, was that he did not prolong any conversation in his usual manner. All questions put to him were answered briefly and to the point.'[18]

At about 8 p.m. he left St Thomas and went to Brighton in St Michael where he met some of his close friends with whom he used to play cards, sometimes bridge but more often poker. Genevieve used to regret his addiction to this pastime because she felt it did nothing at all to relieve the tensions that consumed him from time to time. From Brighton he called her around 9.30 p.m. to see if she was OK and not too lonely.[19]

Then he phoned his mother and they had a long conversation. He seemed to be in no hurry to join his card-playing friends. Perhaps he had a premonition that it was the last time he would talk to the woman who had brought him into this world and whom he cherished with a love that lasted all his life.

He did not return to Ilaro Court until 4 a.m. After four

hours' sleep, he was up and had breakfast with Gen. He did not go to his office that day. He and his wife chatted most of the morning in the study and also had lunch together.

Then Genevieve did something she had never done before. She went to Bridgetown to shop after lunch. During her absence, which lasted less than an hour, Tom went down to the grounds with Cedric Archer of the Ministry of Transport and Works to look at a hole in the fence. On his way back, he spoke with the staff in the kitchen and when he returned to his study he collapsed just inside the door. It seemed amazing to Genevieve that no one found him, since the door was still open when she returned from Bridgetown.[20] She jumped to his side and tried to remember what she had ever known of artificial respiration. But all her efforts to revive him were of no avail.

Then, with a supreme effort, she managed to control herself and called his doctor, William St John, who, after a careful examination, signed a certificate of death due to cardiac failure.[21] Later, Sir Arnott Cato, the acting Governor-General, Dr Trevor Hassell, cardiologist, and Bernard St John, the Deputy Prime Minister, arrived.

Others calling at Ilaro Court were Lady Adams, Maggie Bartlett, a close friend, and Winston Adams, Tom's first cousin. They found Genevieve sitting next to Tom's bed with her hand on his head. She was weeping and her grief seemed unconsolable. The undertaker came and she asked him whether Tom's body could remain with her overnight. She was told that such a thing could not be allowed. As a concession he would allow the body to remain at Ilaro Court until 9 p.m. Actually, it was not taken away until 9.45 p.m.[22]

Genevieve did not expect that such a fate would without warning overtake Tom because he always made light of his heart condition. The suddenness of his death therefore added to her shock and bereavement in her hour of agony. It was clear that, in spite of the turbulence and hazards of politics, she had never ceased to love the extraordinary man she had married twenty-three years before.

Notes

1. J.M.G. Adams, Message of the 14th Anniversary of Independence, delivered on radio and TV, 30 Nov. 1980.
2. *Central Bank of Barbados Annual Report*, 1982.
3. *Central Bank of Barbados Annual Report*, 1983.
4. *Central Bank of Barbados Annual Report*, 1984.
5. Adams' response to the Fifth Meeting of the Conference of the Heads of Government held in Nassau, Bahamas, 4−7 July 1984.
6. Adams at Heads of Government Conference, 4−7 July 1984.
7. Address by J.M.G.M. Adams on the occasion of the official opening of Heywoods and the Speightstown By-pass 18 Jan. 1984.
8. Hansard, 17 April 1984, pp. 957−8.
9. Letter from Dr. C.B. Clarke to the author, 28 Nov. 1986.
10. Letter from Genevieve Adams to the author, 3 Nov. 1986.
11. Related by Genevieve to the author in New York, 22 Oct. 1985.
12. Letter from Genevieve Adams to the author, 3 Nov. 1986.
13. Letter from Genevieve to the author, 3 Nov. 1986.
14. *Advocate*, 10 March 1985.
15. Letter from Genevieve to the author, 3 Nov. 1986.
16. Ibid.
17. Joyce Straker to the author, 15 March 1985.
18. *Nation Keepsake*, 24 March 1985.
19. Letter from Genevieve Adams to the author, 3 November 1986.
20. Ibid.
21. Ibid.
22. Related by Winston Adams to the author, 12 March 1985.

FOURTEEN

Interim Assessment

_____ *1* _____

It would be futile to attempt a final assessment of the career of Tom Adams so soon after his death. Such an assessment must await the release of papers with which one could document important aspects of his life and times. Also of invaluable assistance would be memoirs when they are published by those who knew him more intimately than most of his colleagues.

We refer to such persons as Lady Adams, his mother and Genevieve, his wife, who knew him better than anyone else; Johnny Cheltenham, who can speak of Tom's legacy with understanding and charity; Nigel Barrow, who had a clear view of Tom's philosophy and political strategy; Alair Shepherd, who worked closely with him as a professional colleague; Howard Roberts, who had an intimate knowledge of his shrewdness and assiduity as a political campaigner; and Dolores Hinds and Shirley King, who knew him as well as any of the women who worked with dedication and affection to make his endeavours the undoubted success they were.

These are only some of the many men and women who possessed an intimate knowledge of Tom Adams as a private person and as a public figure. They ought to be interviewed some day to elicit their recollections and to reveal the quantity and the nature of the correspondence Tom Adams conducted with them.

Tom believed in the historical importance of the written word, as a close and familiar friend once said.[1] On the occasion of the 1974 debate on the constitutional amendments, he was careful to read into the record every important submission that was made to him by all the dissenting organisations and persons who had contacted him as Leader of the Opposition.

At the time of the Grenada rescue mission which was sadly misunderstood by Commonwealth leaders, he wrote detailed letters to every single one of them. It is believed that, as a result of this, some of the leaders changed their views.

There are many who can testify to his humanity. If anyone, however humble or however highly placed, achieved anything, he would write him or her a personal letter under his official letterhead. He understood the power of his office to impress or encourage the citizens of the island. Women were almost irresistibly attracted to him and he rejoiced in it; yet to his wife he was a loving and remarkable man who was always warm and caring.

It is generally regarded as a fact that he would reply to every letter that was written to him. Indeed, he was constantly in contact with people of all sorts and it would be a task of some magnitude to have all his correspondence collected and published.

The human side of Tom Adams was evident in another form of communication. He was never reluctant to pick up the telephone and speak to lowly civil servants, if he thought it necessary. He would phone political opponents and speak to them directly, such as the late Horatio Cooke, President of the National Union of Public Workers (NUPW), when negotiations between the Government and the Union were in full swing. He would write to Wendell McClean, the University lecturer, about economic matters whether they were in agreement or disagreement.[2]

For Tom Adams, the practice of law was secondary to his involvement in politics. Because of his strong political partisanship, solicitors, who up to 1972 controlled the major briefs, engaged Tom's services only if clients insisted on this. In this way, he suffered from a discrimination that was similar to, but not as pronounced as, that which his father endured in his time.

2

As a result, Tom never enjoyed the success which his colleagues, Henry Forde and Bernard St John, managed to achieve. Indeed, his law practice was said to be only moderately successful. This in spite of the fact that he was unfailingly courteous to judges and other members of the legal profession. Thus it was that his impressive forensic skills never attained their fullest potential at the Civil Bar.[3]

Tom was not long in realising that both he and Errol Barrow, because of their passionate attachment to politics, were deprived of the opportunity of fully developing their talents at the Civil Bar. It was at his wish that Henry Forde, then Attorney-General, recommended him and Errol Barrow to Her Majesty to be appointed Queen's Counsel. It is interesting to recall that Barrow and Adams were admitted to the Inner Bar on the same morning by the Chief Justice, Sir William Douglas.[4]

Tom Adams was a strange combination of a traditionalist and a socialist. He had great respect for the Court and its traditions, and for Parliament and its traditions as well as for the holders of certain offices. He was a freemason because of the ritual, the tradition and the opportunities for comradeship which the masonic body offered him.

In deference to Chief Justice Douglas's views, he assumed responsibility for the Judiciary. He took the point that the man who held so high a post as Chief Justice should receive instructions, when necessary, not from the Attorney-General but from the Prime Minister of Barbados.

Tom considered that the Barbados Labour Party should maintain continuity with the past. For this reason he included in his first Cabinet Ronald Mapp, whom he regarded as a link with the earlier administrations of Dr H.G. Cummins and his father. Moreover, he systematically rewarded all those who had served the Party in previous years. As we have seen earlier, he was particularly anxious to honour those who had supported his father.

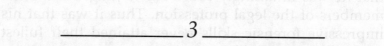

3

His ideals as a socialist were not difficult to discern. One example was his plan for a National Health Service which was his brainchild. Even though it had proved a massive financial burden in the UK, he was resolved to introduce a similar scheme in Barbados. His dream was that the island should be the first country in the developing world to have a plan which would gradually provide a free health service for every man, woman and child, all of whom would be able to go to a doctor of their own choice. The plan, he conceded, would have to be carefully monitored and introduced by stages. In the circumstances in which the scheme was negotiated, however, it could not be achieved.

If heavy taxation is synonymous with socialism, then Tom Adams may well be labelled a socialist. In this respect, he resembled his father in the days when Sir Grantley's slogan was 'soak the rich', particularly during election campaigns in the early years of the labour movement.

One of Tom's first actions as Minister of Finance was to raise the top level of Income Tax to 70 per cent — the highest level it ever reached in Barbados. Later he reduced it to 65 per cent. But under him all taxes were substantially increased. Property Transfer Tax for non-nationals went as high as 17 per cent, though it was reduced later.[5] It should be added, however, that he abolished Estate and Succession duties.

As Minister of Finance, Tom Adams was generally regarded as a great tax collector. He regarded the collection of Land Tax as unsatisfactory when he came to power. He therefore issued instructions that all land taxes prior to 1972 should be officially written off; and he introduced a new system by which land could not be transferred without a Certificate from the Collector of Taxes confirming that all mortgages had been cleared and all previous land taxes had been paid.

Many who knew him well considered him to be parsimonious. In fact, he was as careful in spending his own money as in exacting the strictest accountability in the expenditure of public finances. He realised that, if public money was carefully spent, the burden of taxation could be lightened with justification. It may be mentioned here that, when he visited the UK or the USA, he often arranged his transportation directly with Embassy drivers, much to the irritation of his top diplomats.[6]

Another tax he imposed was the Transport Levy which enabled the Government to fund the massive task of road improvement and reconstruction. Some of his colleagues said that he should have been an engineer in view of the physical developments that followed — the Spring Garden Highway, the St Barnabas

Highway, the Northern Access Road and the road-building feat that was to connect the Deep Water Harbour and the Airport.

4

One of his aims in all this was to realise his vision of Barbados as an off-shore financial centre. It is typical of him that before he died, he had already succeeded in putting into place all the legislation required to bring this dream to reality. Not surprisingly, Erskine Sandiford was later to express the view that Tom Adams was a dreamer and a visionary, grounded in the art of practical politics.[7]

While some thought he should have been an engineer, others among his colleagues seemed to think he should have been a general. To Louis Tull it was one of Tom's regrets that he was not a great military figure, engaged in his strategy and tactics of war.[8] This may well explain the personal interest and support for the Barbados Defence Force. It may also account for the ready support he gave St Vincent in its time of peril and the leading part he played in the Grenada rescue mission.

On his return to Barbados in 1963 Tom was not well known to a wide section of the Barbadian community. It was falsely believed by many that he was a man of limited ability and had benefited from a university education only because his father had created a scholarship for him.[9]

In the years after 1965, as he grew in stature, that image changed completely. They realised that he had not wasted his years in Britain during the period from 1954–62. Indeed, they began to believe that his intellectual powers were greater even than those of his distinguished father.[10]

On a tour of Speightstown with Lionel Craig, MP.

Canvassing.

On his way to deliver the 1982-3 Budget speech, April 1982.

At the BLP Christmas party, 1983.

Reopening the clay preparation plant at Greenland, St Andrew, July 1983.

A Russian-made AK-47 from Grenada, November 1983: Tom with his Chief of Staff.

Senior public officers from the Commonwealth: Tom is in the centre of the front row: on his left is Commonwealth Secretary-General Shridath Ramphal: on Tom's right is Frank Blackman, Barbados Cabinet Secretary.

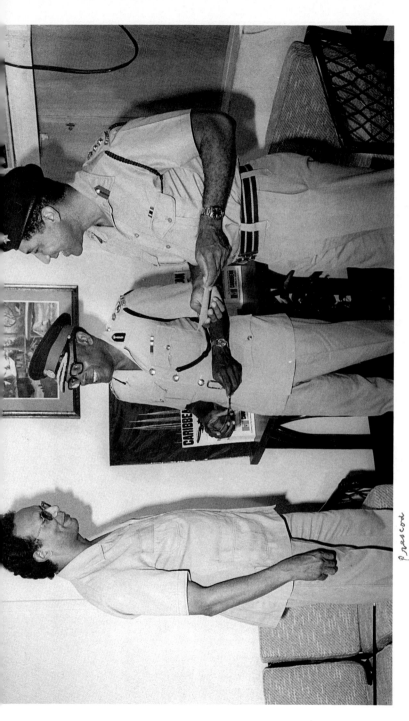

With Police Commissioner Reid and Chief of Staff, Defence Force, Rudyard Lewis.

A final salute.

It was during the City by-election of 1969 that he emerged as a favourite of the crowd. As the campaign progressed, people came to hear him more than anyone else. At that time his speeches were enlivened and enriched with Biblical quotations. With his profound knowledge of the Scriptures and his retentive memory, he developed a facility for adapting passages from Holy Writ to suit many occasions. He used this gift, without any trace of irreverence, to make fun of his opponents and devastate them in argument. From this point, according to a close observer, he became the top political drawing-card on the BLP platform.[11]

As Tom made his way up in the hierarchy of his Party, he seemed to be frequently concerned that someone might be plotting against him. That may be the reason why he usually surrounded himself with a majority of persons who were indubitably his faithful allies. But he never lost the confidence that he could win over those who did not support him. And there can be no doubt that, as he grew into his high office, he towered over possible rivals and lost his suspicion of plotters.[12]

Tom made his way up in the political world by paying the most meticulous attention to detail. His father had taught him that he should reply immediately to every untrue statement. This lesson he took to heart and it is probably true that at times he carried it to the extreme. For he always adhered to the belief that, if some falsehood was not immediately refuted, it could not afterwards be successfully retracted.

Tom's attention to the minutest detail was illustrated in his political campaigning. He used a card-index system in which he recorded the name of every single voter in his constituency of St Thomas. 'If for example,' it has been submitted, 'an elector he recognised heckled him in Porey Spring, an appropriate note might be made on that voter's card. If there was some important fact about the elector − a child in university or in the US for example, that too might be noted. The result was that when the constituent came to his office − even years later − he would use the card to jog his prodigious memory. In his last year, Tom relied to a larger extent on his personal computer.'[13]

Tom's emergence as a dominant personality was due in no small measure to his mastery of television. His training at the BBC had not been in vain. When he was in Opposition, he succeeded in his Budget replies in establishing himself as the man who was adequately equipped to lead the Government of Barbados. What was specially noted by one of his chief opponents, Dr Ritchie Haynes, was that in these presentations he succeeded in changing the vocabulary of political debate in economic matters in Barbados.[14]

There can be no doubt that on every occasion when he met his opposite number he emerged victorious in the field of polemical battle. His performance had a potent influence not only in Barbados but in other islands which were reached by CBC TV. Certainly his instant response in the 1976 Budget and his presentation of cheques to eminent persons from a dubious source will long be remembered as having all the ingredients of high theatre.

With his gambler's instinct, he was passionately fond of poker, liking to win and hating to lose. He carried the same instinct into politics, which was a game that he played to win, using all his intellectual and physical resources to ensure victory. It is not surprising that he won all three by-elections and the two general elections in which he led his Party.

In the St Peter by-election, when the BLP candidate lost by one vote in July 1984, Tom appealed to the courts with the approval of his colleagues. They were confident of his knowledge of the law. But when his appeal was upheld, he was urged by those close to him not to fight Sybil Leacock in another by-election. Tom paid no heed to such advice. He felt that the BLP should not have a defeat recorded against it. Against the counsel of most of his colleagues, he fought the by-election all over again. He was determined to win and he won. He had demonstrated not only that he knew the law but that his political judgement could be trusted.[15]

5

Tom was deeply interested in the Commonwealth Parliamentary Association, was at one time its regional representative and attended all the meetings he could. He believed in the CPA for two reasons. It sought to keep the Commonwealth together and to preserve the ideal of parliamentary democracy.

In 1974, while he was still in opposition, he was selected by the Errol Barrow Government to attend the CPA meeting in Sri Lanka. The Barbados contingent was led by C.E. (now Sir Edwy) Talma, a Government Minister.

Owen T. Allder, who was also a member of the Barbados delegation, has a vivid recollection of Tom's performance on that occasion. He recalls that Tom made brilliant contributions at the Sri Lanka meeting and was always 'out front' in the discussions that took place. His admiration for his fellow-Barbadian was confirmed and strengthened from that day as he followed his strenuous efforts to build the Barbadian infrastructure.

Throughout his two terms of office — the second was never completed — Tom Adams demonstrated a deep sense of commitment to the welfare not only of Barbados but of CARICOM and the Caribbean area.

He was greatly cheered when the Bahamas agreed in 1983 to host the Fifth Meeting of the Conference of Heads of Government of the Caribbean Community. That offer was made immediately after the Nassau Government had demonstrated its commitment to the Caribbean Community by signing and depositing the formal Instrument of Ratification by which it became a full member of CARICOM.

At that meeting Adams expressed the hope that they could all look forward to an even deeper involvement of the Bahamas in the affairs of the Caribbean Community as they worked together to give further impetus to the regional integration movement. He regretted that much water had flowed under the bridge since the Tenth Anniversary Conference in Port-of-Spain. Yet the fact that they had in all the circumstances agreed to meet at Nassau was, he hoped, a happy augury and could indicate that the factors which united them were stronger than those that divided them. He spoke with characteristic realism when he suggested that they should undertake their deliberations with a sense of special urgency and seriousness. He warned that CARICOM and the Caribbean were, for compelling economic and political reasons, more important for them than ever before.[16]

6

Tom Adams had also spoken on several occasions at the conferences on Caribbean Trade, Investment and Development held at Miami, Florida. At the fifth conference held on 1 December 1981, he discoursed on Caribbean development, United States security and the role of development assistance. He was undaunted by the fact that in many parts of the Caribbean it was almost heretical to think that US security interests were the proper concern of the people of the Caribbean. He was equally undaunted by the belief of many Americans that Caribbean development did not and could not contribute significantly to US security.

The Barbados Prime Minister pointed to the success of the Marshall Plan which was adopted, after the Second World War, for the reconstruction of European economies. That plan succeeded in creating a world economy that permitted the emergence of political and social conditions in which free institutions could exist. So successful was the Plan in Western Europe that it was extended to the developing world but there it achieved less than spectacular success.[17]

Adams challenged the celebrated Professor Bauer, who argued in his book *Equality, the Third World and Economic Delusion* that the Marshall Plan succeeded in Europe because it dealt with rehabilitation whereas in the developing countries it had to cope with development. In Europe there were 'the faculties, motivations and institutions' that facilitated the return to prosperity in four years; whereas in the developing world, its economic plight continued after decades of aid, with failure to repay loans that had been obtained on favourable terms and with prospects of indefinite continuation of official aid.[18]

The Prime Minister refuted Professor Bauer's argument by emphasising that nothing like a true Marshall Plan had ever been extended to the developing countries − 4 billion dollars per year over four years for sixteen nations at the prices that prevailed thirty years ago. He expressed strong disagreement with latter-day arguments that reconstruction was suitable for one of the most massive aid efforts in all of recorded history, but that poverty and underdevelopment at the present time must be left only to the market place for alleviation.[19]

Tom then proceeded to emphasise, with inexorable

logic, that one feature of the nature of the US commitment to the Marshall Plan was the perceived need to combat what was considered even then to be a growing communist threat. He asserted that the Caribbean should not have to present evidence of imminent communist subversion before qualifying for US aid to alleviate the social and economic circumstances of the region.[20]

The high regard for Tom's statesmanship was further confirmed when he was invited to address the American Bar Association at the annual general meeting on 6 August 1984, at Chicago, Illinois. On that occasion, Tom took the opportunity to point out that the legal system of Barbados shared with the American Bar Association the same tradition of law; that both the Barbadians and the Americans traced the roots of their legal systems back to Anglo-Saxon times; that they shared the same developments of equity and of law; that the Common Law of England was their mutual heritage and this had implanted in them an abiding respect for the rule of law.[21] It was because he believed in the affinity of the US and Barbados, that Adams gave Ronald Reagan an enthusiastic welcome when the American President visited the island in April 1982.

Having smoothly and eloquently established, as he proceeded in his speech at Chicago, that this affinity was not restricted to the kinship of their legal systems, Adams then disclosed what was the focus of his address — his concern over the new relationship which was expected to arise from the Caribbean Basin Initiative.

That concern was twofold. It referred particularly to the trade benefits to be derived from the CBI as well as to one of the United States' principal objectives — scrutiny of the tax-related activities of persons subject to United States tax.[22]

Adams took the opportunity to highlight areas that were of particular attraction to foreign investors and at the same time to encourage improvements in the legislation involved.[23] He argued that a well-developed infrastructure enhanced the prospects for successful manufacturing operations in Barbados; that a first-class modern airport combined with a well-equipped harbour provided facilities for external trade and passenger movements; that the island had an extensive network of roads and a new modern highway already under construction, which would link all our industrial parks with the airport and harbour; that adequate and reliable supplies of power were available; and not the least important factor for successful manufacturing operations was that Barbados was a centre of telecommunications in the Caribbean and was equipped with direct telephone dialling worldwide, full telex, and facsimile facilities and the International Data Access System.[24]

Tom also proclaimed his intention to continue his efforts to establish Barbados as a reputable offshore financial centre. As such, the island would seek to attract legitimate financial institutions which needed an offshore location to facilitate their tax-planning or access to markets not readily manageable from a home base.[25] For this purpose Adams entered a strong plea for the restoration of the benefits which Barbados formerly enjoyed from the United States Double Taxation Treaty with the United Kingdom.

Unaware of the fact that he had only seven more months to live and making light of his cardiac condition, Tom Adams continued to press for the realisation of his dream that Barbados would move forward from being a 'non-industrial' to being an 'industrialising economy.'[26]

7

That programme of development was not an end in itself but a means to maximise the benefits that could be received by the people of Barbados and the Caribbean. It was advocated at annual general meetings of the World Bank and the International Monetary Fund. It was the message that Adams relayed, with all the resources of his persuasive eloquence, to the major cities in the UK, Europe, Canada, the USA and Japan. And he never relaxed his efforts until a few days before his death.

Tom may not have won the love of the masses as his father and Errol Barrow had done. He was perhaps too much of an intellectual to have attracted the near-idolatry of his predecessors. He was a man who loved art. He had an intimate and detailed knowledge of art history. He had studied ancient civilisations and would talk with ease and facility of the Assyrian Kingdom or the Babylonian Empire. He was convinced that the treasures of art, music and literature, the annals of history and the voices of philosophers were a vast source of knowledge waiting to be tapped for the benefit of himself, his island home, and the wider Caribbean community.[27] Such a man may not have attained the charisma that springs from an overwhelmingly popular adoration. Yet he compelled the admiration and respect of all who knew his outstanding intellectual qualities.[28]

The Jesuit priest, the Rev. J.F. Besant, in the midst of the sharpest controversies, would refer to Sir Grantley Adams as 'mon cher ami, l'ennemi' — my dear friend, the enemy. That sentiment was reciprocated by Sir Grantley. It had its genesis in the respect one doughty adversary had for the other. In the same way, it may be said that a similar spirit was shared by two of the most formidable opponents in the island's recent political history. For Tom Adams and Errol Barrow, in spite of their many confrontations in the political arena, both respected and admired the special qualities each of them possessed.

Errol Barrow died on 1 June 1987. Like Sir Grantley, it has been written, Barrow upheld integrity in public office with the happy result that Barbados today is not wracked by the scandals of corruption that have besieged Trinidad and Tobago and the Bahamas.[29] Like Errol Barrow, Tom Adams was a politician who turned statesman and gave to his career a dignity and prestige that could well be emulated in other territories of the Caribbean.

Another university professor expressed his view of the three most celebrated men in the recent history of Barbados — Sir Grantley Adams, Tom Adams and Errol Barrow. The professor recalled the days when the parliaments of small Caribbean democracies were enlivened and enriched with 'monumental parliamentary duels of rhetoric and metaphor' between the likes of Alexander Bustamante and Norman Manley in Jamaica, and went on to mention the battles that were fought between Errol Barrow and Sir Grantley Adams and later between Barrow and Grantley's son, Tom. To him these exchanges clearly indicated that democracy would survive in the Caribbean.[30]

Inevitably, some attempt is being made to assess the contributions of the three Barbadians within the circumstances of their times. One interim assessment divides the last fifty years into three periods — struggle, nationalism and realism.[31]

The first was dominated by Grantley Adams, who launched a progressive movement firmly established on a proletarian basis and sought to establish regional independence through a federation of the West Indies.

The second was led by Errol Barrow who, after the dissolution of the WI Federation and the failure to establish a Federation of the Eight, resolved to complete the process of decolonisation started by his predecessor, by proceeding to independence for Barbados alone. Yet he vindicated himself against the charge of insularity by joining with Guyana and Antigua to form a Caribbean Free Trade Area (CARIFTA) which paved the way for CARICOM.

The third was represented by Tom Adams, a transitional figure, who shared the ideals of his two predecessors, and attempted to bring to reality the philosophy of social democracy, as a Barbadian and a Caribbean man, by combining the methods of the visionary and the pragmatist.

Notes

1. Memorandum from Fred Gollop to the author, 19 March 1987, p. 3.
2. Ibid., p. 3.
3. Ibid.
4. Ibid., p. 1.
5. Ibid., p. 2.
6. Ibid.
7. Hansard, 18 March 1985, p. 2094.
8. Ibid., p. 2076.
9. Gollop, op. cit., p. 4.
10. Ibid.
11. Ibid.
12. Henry Forde to the author, 22 March 1987.
13. Gollop, op. cit., p. 3.
14. Hansard, 18 March 1985, p. 2080.
15. Dick Walcott to the author, 1 December 1984.
16. Adams' address to the Fifth Meeting of the Conference of Heads of Government of the Caribbean Community, Nassau, the Bahamas, 4–7 July 1984, pp. 1–2.
17. Adams' address at Miami Conference, 1 December 1981, pp. 4–5.
18. Ibid.
19. Ibid.
20. Ibid., p. 5.
21. Adams' Address to the American Bar Association 6 August 1984, pp. 1–2.
22. Ibid., p. 2.
23. Ibid., p. 3.
24. Ibid., p. 9.
25. Ibid., p. 12.
26. Ibid., p. 9.
27. Hansard, House of Assembly debates, 18 March 1985, pp. 2076, 2078.
28. Ibid.
29. Professor Gordon Lewis, 'Barrow: A Quiet Revolutionary', *Sunday Nation*, 7 June 1987.
30. Professor Anthony P. Maingot, *Miami Herald*, 12 June 1987.
31. Dr Neville Duncan, Senior Lecturer in Political Science, Cave Hill Campus, UWI, speaking as a member of a panel on CBC TV, 7 June 1987.

FIFTEEN

The Verdict of the Elected Representatives

1

The first rumour of Tom Adams' death started just after three o'clock on the afternoon of 11 March 1985. Barbadians of all walks of life tried to find out if it was true. They simply could not believe that the Prime Minister, who was at the height of his physical and intellectual powers, would no longer be seen walking about the streets of Bridgetown or driving through the rural areas of the country.

The state of uncertainty lasted for more than an hour. All the telephone lines at Government Headquarters were jammed and officials could only say that they had no confirmation of the rumour that was spreading all over the island. Eventually, it was officially announced at 4.30 p.m. that the Prime Minister had died suddenly at his official residence, Ilaro Court, on Two Mile Hill, in St Michael.

To some it was bitter news to hear, resulting in a state of almost unbearable shock. Some wept openly and unashamedly. A stunned and solemn atmosphere seemed to spread throughout the island. Yet a persistent spirit of scepticism prevailed on all sides and people appeared to be saying silently to themselves: 'It can't be true. It is impossible.'

For three days the body of the late Prime Minister lay in state in the East wing of Parliament Buildings.

The people were still stunned and stricken with grief as they waited in their thousands in the street and in the precincts of Parliament to view the body of the man who had led the island for more than eight years with courage, resource and intelligence.

The state funeral was held on Saturday, 16 March. It was attended by representatives of forty-six countries — twelve from all the CARICOM territories and thirty-four from nations of the world beyond the Caribbean region. Significantly a special delegation came from Grenada, the island Tom had played a major part in rescuing from the brutalities of an alien ideology.

As Adams left Ilaro Court for the last time, the cortège was accompanied by an impressive procession. People watched or followed it all the way as it proceeded to the Prime Minister's last resting-place in the graveyard of St Michael's Cathedral. The crowds along the way could not believe that the sound of the voice which once fascinated them was now forever stilled. Some were silent; with others, their lamentation was like cries countless, cries like dead letters sent to him who lived no more.

One piece of music which was much loved by Tom Adams was played at the funeral by the Cathedral organist, Dr John Fletcher. It was Dvorak's New World Symphony. At the special request of Genevieve, the music was found after some difficulty and incorporated in the service. A member of the British delegation present at the funeral later confessed how deeply moved he was to hear Dvorak's Symphony played for the first time in his experience in the New World.

2

In the meantime, the mass of ordinary people expressed their grief over the passing of their Prime Minister in

162

their own various ways. Some mourned because they would no longer feel the touch of a vanished hand. Others because they would no longer hear the sound of the voice that was still. Others again mourned the loss of the statesman who, immediately after he became Prime Minister and Minister of Finance, introduced an austerity budget because of the threatening outlook of the world economic situation and was rewarded by a steady improvement in the Barbadian economy.[1]

In the meantime the news had spread to distant parts of the world. In far-off Toronto a young Barbadian woman on holiday was purchasing essential supplies in one of the shops in that city. Just before she was about to pay for her goods, a radio placed in a high corner of the shop announced that Tom Adams of Barbados was dead. Immediately, big round tears coursed one another down her innocent cheeks, as if in piteous chase. The shop assistant, touched by her emotion, sought to soothe her anguish by saying: 'Miss, if you don't have sufficient money to pay for these things, please don't worry, it's not the end of the world.' To this she replied: 'It's not that: it has just been announced that my Prime Minister is dead.'[2]

The mood of the whole country was expressed by the *Nation* in the following excerpt from its editorial:

We feel, like the poet, Shelley, who on the death of his friend, John Keats, in the prime of life, penned these immortal words:
I weep for Adonais — he is dead!
O, weep for Adonais! though our tears
Thaw not the frost that binds so dear a head!
And thou, sad Hour, selected from all years
To mourn our loss, rouse thy obscure compeers,
And teach them thine own sorrow, say:
'With me died Adonais; till the Future
Dares forget the past, his fate and fame

Shall be an echo and a light unto eternity!
Tom Adams is dead. We shall not see his like again.[3]

It is still too early, as suggested earlier, to attempt a final assessment of the career of Tom Adams. We must content ourselves with the verdict of the Parliament of Barbados — a verdict that was expressed in the House of Assembly and the Senate.

3

The new Prime Minister, Bernard St John, said that in all his experience he knew no one who loved parliamentary democracy more than Tom Adams. He knew of no one else who was more interested in preserving the Westminister system of government. He helped in a large measure to shape the Constitution, the fundamental instrument which governs the people of Barbados.

He was a Caribbean man who shared the deep disappointment of his colleagues and his father over the demise of the Federation of the West Indies. He had a clear vision of the need for mutual self-help in all areas of the Caribbean and nowhere was this more firmly manifested than when he played a major role in the Grenada rescue mission.

No one was better qualified than the new Prime Minister to speak of Tom's determination to salvage what he could from the wreckage of the defunct Federation. He never doubted that an association, if not a formal legal, political union, would one day undertake many of the functions that the Federation had hoped to perform.

St John knew the price Tom Adams had to pay for his loyalty to the ideal of Caribbean unity. He bore the brunt of criticism because of Barbados' position in regard to the Multilateral Clearing Facility. But he stood firm because he was convinced that Barbados' policy on the Facility was totally consistent with his view of the role Barbados should play in the Caribbean. There were many who regarded the stance of Tom Adams and his Government as unduly generous but he was confident that Barbados was destined to play a pivotal role in the process of reconstructing suitable instruments for effecting Caribbean association.

St John went on to say:

He knew that one cannot always receive benefits without having to bear burdens, and there can be no doubt that the progress Barbados has made in many areas of its economic activity, particularly in the manufacturing area, during the course of his tenure of office as Prime Minister of this country from 1976 until his death, was made because of the fact that we were part of the Caribbean Economic Community, and that our people were able to rise to the challenge presented by the limited Common Market opportunities. Statistics will show and demonstrate that Barbados, above all, benefited greatly from the Common Market.[4]

4

No one had more reason than Brandford Taitt to resent the castigation he had at times received from Tom Adams in the House of Assembly. On one occasion he was sharply criticised for the methods in which he controlled prices as Minister of Trade. He was told that, while he aimed at reducing the cost of living by his controls, he succeeded in emptying the shelves of the island's shops and supermarkets. With a cruel lash of his tongue, Adams advised the Government of the day to make Taitt Minister of Garbage and all the garbage that disgraced Bridgetown and other parts of the country would disappear.

Nevertheless, as chief spokesman for the Opposition, he acted in the highest tradition of the parliamentary system when he seconded the Resolution of Sympathy moved by the Prime Minister. He agreed with St John when he said that, if Tom Adams was anything at all, he was a parliamentarian.

One of the things which impressed the Opposition member was the unfailing courtesy which Tom Adams exercised in the course of debate. At the height of the most perfervid debate, one only had to rise in one's seat and say the oft-repeated words 'On a point ...' the late Prime Minister never waited to hear what the word was before he took his seat and permitted the member to say what he wanted to say. To Brandford Taitt that was not a trivial matter. It represented one of the most important aspects of the parliamentary system which Barbados had inherited more than 300 years ago.

The honourable member expressed his admiration for Tom Adams as a debater. He confessed that at times he himself was at the brunt of Adams' wit and in his own time he had tried to 'accost' him in similar terms. However, he conceded that when Adams the debater was in full cry, even those who were at the mercies of his tongue could not help but notice the facility with which he phrased what he had to say.

Brandford Taitt also claimed the distinction of having battled with Tom Adams the campaigner. He could not think of a more indefatigable and committed campaigner. He had locked horns with him in two by-elections, St Michael South Central and St Peter. In both of those campaigns, his unfailing commitment to his own party, to his own ideals and to what he perceived to be the only ultimate result was transparently clear to all who saw him in action and all who 'felt the brunt of his tremendous wit'.

The Opposition member continued:

> Mr Speaker, the people of Barbados have spoken eloquently of their views of the Prime Minister's death and the Prime Minister himself, but I think that it can be said again that whenever one hears of and experiences a death in the way in which we experienced the death of a man who was at the height of his powers, who appeared at the height of his vigour, and who was cut down in the morning, it must humble us politicians. It must reduce us and teach us humility, because we become closely familiar with a statement which is heard from the Good Book time and time again that the days of man are but as grass − the grass withers and the flowers thereof fadeth away.

5

To Louis Tull, then Attorney-General, Tom Adams not only 'bestrode this Parliament like a Colossus', and showed remarkable powers of advocacy at the Bar, he was also a great historian who read every book on the history of Barbados and quoted frequently and liberally from all the historical works relating to the island.

His interest in history spread far and wide. He was particularly fond of military history and could speak in great detail of military figures leading large forces into battle. He could talk knowledgeably of the wars of the Greeks, the Romans and the Carthaginians. He seemed to know what were the particular strengths of Hannibal, the particular weaknesses of Caesar and the qualities that made Alexander the Great the celebrated leader that he was. Moreover, he had a knowledge of German military history which Tull believed was second to none.

Louis Tull and Tom Adams shared an interest in philosophy from Plato and Aristotle right through the middle part of this century up to the philosophers of modern times. They would exchange views on the modern existentialist philosophers and Tull was amazed how the Prime Minister could find time to master the details of extremely complex political and philosophical thought.

Tull confessed that he had fought a number of 'classic' battles with Tom. He had clashed with the late Prime Minister both in the Government and in the Party. Tom fought him with the fierceness that he fought his political opponents but at the end they would appreciate their respective positions. Tull emphasised this because he did not want it to be felt that Tom enjoyed a close relationship only with flatterers, those who would lap up every word that fell from his lips. In fact, it was those who fought and resisted him who in the end had the greatest respect for him.

Dr R. L. Cheltenham recalled that God had blessed Tom with a robust and many-sided intellect which he assiduously cultivated by constant reading. His taste was catholic, including biographies, autobiographies, social histories, military affairs, cricket, gardening, stamp-collecting and art. His oratory in the House and on the political platform was powerful and overwhelming. He could be pungent and witty, stringent and combative, and, when aroused in debate, ruthless and irascible. Yet it will long be remembered that as a leader of men, he was generous, compassionate, wise and supportive. He gave to the high office of state he held, the indelible stamp of his character — restless energy, mastery of concept and detail, dynamism, probity and vision.

As a regionalist, Dr Cheltenham added, Tom walked in the footsteps of his illustrious father and was uncompromisingly committed to the regional economic movement. There was little doubt that nothing brought him more distress than the decline in regional trade, the collapse of the Multilateral Clearing Facility and the general 'logjam' of the moment. He loved life, the honourable member concluded, and lived it to the limit of his enormous energy.[5]

———————— 6 ————————

Dr R.C. Haynes had cause, like Brandford Taitt, to remember the furious torrent of Tom Adams' eloquence. In one of his Budget speeches Tom attempted with scathing sarcasm, to castigate the honourable member for the manner in which he dealt with serious economic problems. It was a blow below the belt and delivered mercilessly and without pity. But Haynes accepted it as part of the give and take of debate.

After his death Haynes spoke of the late Prime Minister in the same magnanimous terms as his Opposition colleague, Brandford Taitt. He said that the death of Tom Adams was a tragic loss for the democratically elected Parliament of the country, for his political party and for the nation as a whole. Above all, he knew it was a tragic loss to his wife, his two sons, Douglas and Rawdon, to his mother, Lady Adams, and to his relatives.

Dr Haynes and the late Prime Minister had had their sharp differences on national economic policy but this never prevented him from appreciating the qualities that made Tom Adams so formidable an opponent. Dr Haynes said:

I have chosen to speak of Mr Adams, the parliamentarian, whose gifts as the Member for St Thomas found full expression, and who did much by style and content to shape the pattern of debate in this House. To me, his passing is a tragic loss. I have enjoyed many battles with him, some won, some lost, but at all times we understood the difference between relentless debate in pursuit of a cause, which he espoused, and general hate and animosity, which are destructive of human respect. And so it was that before and after the most bitter of exchanges, we could still exchange a view on that or any other matter relating to Barbados.[6]

7

Henry Forde declared that it was not usual for people to look in the face of God. But he was sure that many of them did that during the past few days.

Many of us would have asked why not one of us or some other less capable person than Tom Adams. There was no doubt that Tom Adams was perhaps the most dynamic leader that we have witnessed in Barbados for a long time. In some respects his leadership has probably surpassed that of his great father.

Forde spoke of Tom's commitment to his country. It was obvious that Tom, with such an illustrious father, found a great deal of resentment among some people who 'grudged' him. Although honourable members were paying tribute to his memory, Forde was not prepared to mince words. It was obviously not easy for Tom to return to Barbados when he realised that some people wanted to settle scores with his father against him personally. Yet Tom realised the wider duty he had to the people of Barbados and he therefore threw himself unreservedly into the political life of this country.

It is now past history, that when we were defeated again in 1971 most of us, as the Attorney-General has said, were totally deflated, dejected and depressed. In this House it was Tom Adams' voice that spoke to many of us and reminded us of the serious commitment which we had to our Party to help rebuild it, with the long-term national goal of carrying on the great work for which our Party was founded.

Forde reminded the House that the slogan used against Tom Adams, when he led the BLP in 1976, was 'Can you trust Tom Adams?' Forde expressed the conviction that Tom's life and performance proved beyond measure that he was totally trustworthy and capable. He wished this to stick in the minds of Barbadians because they were apt to praise their heroes only when they had passed to the Great Beyond.[7]

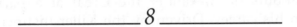

8

Billie Miller, to whom had been entrusted the responsibilities for the arrangements of the State funeral, spoke of Tom's loyalty to friends and colleagues. He was particularly generous with words. He never missed a chance to praise both with the spoken and the written word. He loved to write, whether it was a letter of gratitude, of praise, of congratulation or of condolence. His letter-writing was part of the romance he had with language.

He was generous too, with his gestures, Miss Miller

added, reaching out to people physically with the pressure of his hand, a handshake or a nod. He could be
generous even with a simple glance and that twinkle
in the eyes, sometimes mischievous.

I believe one of his most wonderful gifts, his most
wonderful physical gift, because many of his gifts
have been extolled over the past seven days, apart
from his bearing as a man and as a Prime Minister,
was his voice. His voice had a timbre, I think it was
not given to any of us; the modulation and his
command of the language. It was something that no
one else, I think, enjoyed. His speech, his oratory,
commanded the ear of those who listened and,
more importantly, I think, that something which is
given to very few people was given to Tom Adams,
and that was the music of language.[8]

9

Erskine Sandiford had also endured the pitiless lash of
Tom's tongue. On one occasion he was challenged, in
spite of his erudite knowledge of the subject as to the
whereabouts of Alexander the Great at a particular
time in his career. Driven by the Killer instinct, Tom
tried to ridicule him before the large audience
provided by television. Yet the memory of the past
did not prevent Sandiford from delivering a cool and
balanced review of Tom's career at the time of his
death.

Speaking for the Opposition, Sandiford regretted
that 'neither storied urn nor animated bust' could
restore Tom Adams to them. He did not share the
view that domestic politics was the pursuit of civil
war by other means. He did not believe that to move a
country forward they had to use all the weapons in the

military arsenal in order to get things done. This approach to public affairs encouraged the worst aspects of human nature and appealed to hatred, to venom and to other Machiavellian pursuits.

On the contrary, he believed that in discussing the serious issues facing a country, they could have different outlooks, visions, goals and objectives, that they could have different methods and techniques of arriving at those objectives. Sandiford believed that, in a mature democracy,they could debate matters in the true spirit of democracy, arrive at decisions and respect those decisions until time and circumstances called for a review of those decisions. That, he believed, was the essence of parliamentary democracy.

He then spoke of Tom Adams as one who believed in parliamentary democracy. He expressed the view that the late Prime Minister's work in Parliament was a tribute to that democracy.

I also believe that Tom Adams was a dreamer and a visionary and it is not for me on this occasion to speak on or to reflect on his visions and his dreams. He was grounded in *réal politique*, (sic) the arts of practical politics, but he was also a visionary and a dreamer. Perhaps when the time comes for a balanced assessment of his contribution, it will be seen that perhaps it was his visionary nature and his dreams that were even more important than the practical contributions which he made to the Government and politics of this country.[9]

Perhaps the most touching speech was made by the latest addition to the House, Owen Arthur. The latter had worked with the late Prime Minister in a professional capacity for two years in the Ministry of Finance and Planning. He confessed that to work with Tom Adams was 'a very stirring test of the intellect' because he had a 'painstaking regard for proper method'. He was noted for 'a great insistence on accuracy' and above all he was inspired by 'a great passion for clear and clean decisions'. Arthur added that:

> to work with him was also to be caught up in the excitement of a great economic adventure as he sought to steer this country in a new direction through the monumental work he put into our new Five Year Plan. But I recall that in all this, no matter how stern were the tasks and how difficult those decisions that he had to take, Tom Adams was a man of humanity and humility, for none of his subordinates in the Ministry of Finance and Planning can ever recall an angry word or a raised voice during the difficult economic years over which he had to preside.

Arthur continued to speak with a personal touch that made his speech almost unique.

Many persons in this Chamber today speak of Mr Adams as a political colleague. I perhaps can speak more personally of him as something of a political father because it was through his personal inspiration and encouragement that I took the decision to enter public life. I will always gratefully and very fondly remember the efforts he made to transfer this encouragement to me into success on my account. In the political struggles that he fought on my behalf, there was no burden that was too large for him to bear. He was the mastermind of my political campaign, but he also found the time to be a convasser as well. In his very complete way, he found time both to be my general as well as one of my foot soldiers.[10]

10

One important thing need to be added here. Before paying his tribute in the House, Dr Richard Haynes stated that the leader of the Opposition, Errol Barrow, had asked him to be most 'meticulous' to indicate that it was only because of the fact that he was suffering from acute laryngitis that he was not present in the Chamber that day and despite that he made every effort to attend the State Funeral.

Errol Barrow took the opportunity to express his views in the Press. He said that Tom Adams was more of a politician than his father, the legendary Sir Grantley Adams. He was 'the most political animal' we have had over the last 75 years. He enjoyed every minute as a politician. Errol Barrow declared that he himself did it out of a sense of duty, but to Tom Adams it was not only a vocation, but a calling. It was a game he enjoyed. 'A lot of us in public life', added Barrow, 'wish to be doing something else, but not Mr Adams. He was 100 per cent politician.'

The Leader of the Opposition concluded his statement by expressing the view that the Barbados Labour Party would not be the same without Tom Adams. Whether it was meant at the time to be prophetic it is difficult to say. It will be remembered that in 1974 Barrow had publicly confessed that he could not beat Adams in the House because he was too clever. Barrow added that he could only beat him in elections. But after Tom's three by-election victories in 1976 and 1984 and his two general election triumphs in 1976 and 1981, Barrow may have begun to wonder about that, too.

After Tom's death, Barrow may have begun to look to the future of his Democratic Labour Party with a greater measure of confidence and certainty. It may well be, therefore, that his remarks on 24 March 1985, were ominous for the BLP and prophetic for the DLP. Certainly this is one way of explaining Errol Barrow's resounding victory at the polls fourteen months after the death of Tom Adams.

Notes

1. *The Times*, 23 March 1985.
2. Wendy Hoyos to the author, 11 March 1985.
3. *Nation Keepsake*, 24 March 1985.
4. Hansard, 18 March 1985, pp. 272–3.
5. Ibid., pp. 2078–9.
6. Ibid., pp. 2079–81.
7. Hansard, 18 March 1986, pp. 2085–7.
8. Hansard, 28 March 1986, pp. 2090–92.
9. Hansard, 18 March 1985, pp. 2093–4.
10. Ibid., p. 2100.

SIXTEEN

Death Shall Have No Dominion

1

In the preceding chapter we dealt mainly with the speeches made by some of the elected representatives of the people. Equally generous and eloquent tributes were paid in the Senate. Though the latter is constituted in a different way from the House of Assembly, it states the views of important sections of the community, as represented by the Government, the Opposition and Independent Members.

For Nigel Barrow, Leader of the Senate, Monday, 11 March 1985 was a day he would never forget. Earlier that day he received a message from the Prime Minister confirming that he would unveil the emancipation statue on the following Sunday and intended to make a speech. As Minister of Information and Culture, Barrow made a mental note that he would phone the Prime Minister later that day and discuss the matter with him.

Meetings of one sort or another went on during the whole morning and early in the afternoon. Then he went from his office to the Conference Room where the Cabinet was to meet to discuss the Estimates. There he received the chilling news that Tom Adams was dead. Members of the Cabinet sat in silence in their seats and an appallingly gloomy atmosphere prevailed in the Conference Room. Barrow, like his fellow members, knew he had lost a trusted colleague and a close friend.

Barrow said in the Senate a week later,

I knew Tom Adams as a leader of men, decisive, bold and imaginative, thoughtful and compassionate. His hand was firm but gentle. His style of leadership, as his entire career in public life, benefited from his outstanding personal qualities ... the truth was that he hated too see people suffer. It was this concern that led him to provide for the aged and disadvantaged in our society by enhancing pensions and providing services.'[1]

Nigel Barrow considered that Tom Adams' greatest disappointment would have been that he went to his grave before the National Health Service was implemented for all Barbadians. Another great disappointment would have been that he did not live to witness and direct the construction of the major roadworks programme which he saw as vital for two reasons — the economic reconstruction of the island and the provision of work for the unemployed. Barrow continued:

I often heard it said of Tom Adams when he was alive that he tried to achieve too much, he was ahead of his time, he tried to move Barbados forward at too fast a pace. If any of this is true, it is probably because he knew he had so much to do and feared he had not enough time in which to do it. What is true is that he drove himself at a ferocious pace. He demanded hard work and excellence of his colleagues, but he saw no sacrifice as being too great to make for his people. Ultimately, he gave his life in the service of his country.[2]

2

Evelyn Greaves, who spoke for the Opposition, lauded Adams as a dominant figure in his Party, his Cabinet, in Parliament and the country. Greaves believed that the late Prime Minister was one of the most fortunate and well-endowed Barbadians of the century, better endowed than anyone in the island's Parliament, in fact. 'His family circumstances were propitious,' Greaves said, 'mixed and solidly middle-class. His father was a brilliant lawyer, a leader already worshipped as a champion by the broad masses of the people, even if hated by the entrenched wealthy and power holders ... '.

The Opposition member added that in his domestic environment, Tom Adams was exposed early to the world of politics and public affairs and to the clash of sharp and mature intellects. He accepted the theory of educationists that such exposure influenced one's development in later life. 'Adams' own inherently sharp intellect, his disposition for hard work and his attention to detail only enhanced those positive aspects of his career.'

Greaves declared that Adams was fortunate to be able to pursue his goals for good living and public affairs.

There may be very few persons alive in Barbados today who have visited the Eastern Bloc, far less the seat of Communism, Moscow. Tom Adams was able to do this over twenty years ago. He had no need, like most of us, to hurry his education, since it can be seen that he was carefully preparing himself for the role he was to play in the political life of Barbados and the wider Caribbean. So his education was not only the formal part of the university but also to life in the wider world.[3]

Canon Ivor Jones, an Independent Member, was moved to quote from Mark Anthony's speech on the death of Julius Caesar.

> Oh, what a fall was there my countrymen!
> Then I and you, and all of us fell down ...

The majority of Barbadians, I am sure, had the gut feeling that so long as Tom Adams was Prime Minister of this country, whatever might be the slings and arrows of outrageous fortune that beset us, be it the IMF, the recession or the Marxist attempt at overthrowing democracy in this region, our confidence in his ability, farsightedness and expertise to meet those challenges and surmount them remained steadfast and inviolable.

The Canon was as proud as all Barbadians to hear the comments from all the West Indian leaders as well as from the President of the United States and the Prime Ministers of Great Britain and Canada who had all been impressed by Tom Adams' 'massive intellect and comprehensive grasp of social, political and economic problems.'[4]

3

O'Brian Trotman, a Government Member, who claimed to be one of Tom's closest friends, could vouch for the fact that Adams was a man who took time off from his duties as a Prime Minister to return every telephone call that was made to him, paying no regard to who was the caller. If he could not answer the same day he would telephone the next day with an apology for not returning the call the day before. He was as easily at home with the ordinary man or woman as he was with a visiting Head of State. Trotman recalled:

I well remember his entertaining a visiting CPA team at Alexandra's for dinner. After the formalities, Tom decided he was going to have some fun because he was a fun-loving man, and when the senior Parliamentarian from Britain turned to me and said, 'Certainly, the Prime Minister is not going into that crowd', I said, 'Just you wait and see.' Tom left us, went across the floor and led a young lady from a completely different generation on to the floor and proceeded to take over the disco floor at Alexandra's. He knew how to live.[5]

Wendall McClean, an Independent Member, could not claim to be as intimate a friend of Tom Adams as some of the earlier speakers. Yet from what he had observed he could entirely agree with what had been said of the late Prime Minister. In the circumstances in which he had to lead Barbados, McClean identified as Adams' outstanding attributes his thoroughly professional and scientific approach to politics, his inclination to operate on the basis of careful analysis rather than on whim or prejudice, his open-mindedness and his recognition that any view of any reasonable person must be essentially a tentative view, subject to change in the light of further evidence. McClean believed that those qualities had resulted in great benefit to Barbados in terms of the decisions which he had to make in this country.

McClean, an economist of high repute, remembered that, when Adams came to office, he was faced with Barbados on the verge of severe balance of payment problems, and on the advice of his official advisers the late Prime Minister had taken up the notion that he must accept a policy of wage restraints and various measures such as import controls. The economist spoke out against much of this and he indicated the level of wage settlements that Barbados could endure. In the case of the Secondary Teachers Union he told them what they should ask for and he offered Adams the same advice. McClean went on:

> It is a matter of history that they got what they asked for. At the time, I told him in a letter, touching on the matter, that the only difference between the Ministry of Finance under the Barbados Labour Party at that time and the Ministry of Finance under the Democratic Labour Party was the Minister of Finance and, if he relied entirely on the advice of his officials, he would be relying on exactly what his predecessor in office relied on, and the consequences would be exactly the same. So he had to rise above that situation if Barbados was to go forward. I must say that he did this in a most excellent manner.[6]

4

Clyde Griffith, a Government Member, regarded the death of Tom Adams as a personal loss. He shared the privilege of those few people who spent many evenings with him after long days of hard work. They would talk in his office far into the night, conversing about life, politics, about his vision for Barbados and the Caribbean and about world affairs.

During the four years he served as Consul-General in New York, Griffith became a close friend of Tom Adams. The occasions when the late Prime Minister came to New York were regarded as the highlights of his term of office as Consul-General. The Senator added:

> I doubt very much that many people knew how much he loved New York as a city. For him New York was a place where you could come and relax, go to the theatre, shop, take in the beauty of the city, the museums and the other attractions. Many a

day he and I would go for very long walks and I learned about New York City from him in those days. He used to teach me about its history, where estates were in Manhattan and about the layout of the City; all of those things you could not get from reading in books about New York, he could impart to you because he knew the City so well and he loved the City dearly.[7]

Clarence Jemmott, a Government Member, emphasised that, contrary to what some people thought and said about him, Tom was one of the most forgiving persons he had ever met. The Caribbean and the world had lost a great man. It was always his desire, as it had been his father's, to have 'a fully well-knit Caribbean community'. It was always his desire that we in the Caribbean should live as one people. Jemmott expressed agreement with Wes Hall, who had spoken before him, that, if those of them who were left would strive to achieve that objective, they would have done his name proud. He added that he regarded Adams not only as a Caribbean man but also as an international figure.[8]

5

Perhaps the outstanding speech in the Senate was that of Mrs Enid Lynch, an Independent Member. She could not claim close acquaintance with him as other speakers had done. Her recollection of him would always be 'inextricably entangled' with her impression of his parents, Sir Grantley and Lady Adams who were closer to her generation. She had more contact with them at an exciting and challenging period in the development of Barbados. At that time Grace Thorne was a young teacher at St Michael's Girls' School until she married the courageous young lawyer, Grantley Adams. 'I therefore joined the lusty cheers' said the Senator, 'which expressed the relief and joy with which we hailed the news that Tom had at last arrived safely in this world and that his mother was out of danger.'

Mrs Lynch thought that the early life of Tom Adams was an interesting study of the making of a Caribbean statesman. He inherited much from the brilliance and courage of his father and the affection and wisdom of his mother. He must have gathered much not only from their conversation but from the splendid library at Tyrol Cot. He had the advantage of meeting the great crusading politicians of Barbados and the other territories of the Caribbean and many of the outstanding figures from the outside world.

He would also have met 'the budding trade unionists', Hugh Springer, Frank Walcott, Mencea Cox and other pioneers. He learnt something of real life as he played with the many youngsters in the neighbourhood of Tyrol Cot. He would have known the realities of life especially during the dark days of the 1937 riots and was somewhat caught up in the events of that time.

He would have seen many simple people at Tyrol Cot coming to his father to ask for some favour or to report some grievance. In Enid Lynch's opinion, the son was even more charming than his father. From all the circumstances of his environment, he acquired that faith in the common sense of simple people who felt that the son was as accessible as the father.

'I think that a great political party,' continued Mrs Lynch, 'remains great in defeat and it was when Tom Adams led a group of seven Opposition parliamentarians between 1971 and 1976 that my admiration for him became greater than something based on childhood memories. The fighting spirit, the debating skills, the knowledge which that small group of parliamentarians showed made their strength appear far greater than their numbers would have suggested.'

Though Tom Adams had to bear many heavy pressures, to her he seemed to carry them with considerable self-control and sometimes even with humour. He was constantly faced with a series of crises, beginning with the Cubana disaster which destroyed the lives of the entire crew and passengers — a tragedy that occurred even before he had settled down to the business of government.

Mrs Lynch recalled the Grenada crisis of 1983 for which he could rely on no precedent.

That was a particularly testing time, and the entire Caribbean area became unsettled. If his weak heart ever faltered, he never showed it with pressures of these kinds. I must admit that I was not entirely surprised that his brilliance, his charm, all the great promise which he had, was not supported by an equally strong physique. He had the courage to make unpopular decisions. As we praise him, let us remember those occasions when he was a very unpopular Prime Minister because he dared to make the decisions which he thought were to the ultimate benefit of his country. He could not truthfully be accused of failing to do what was right for the country because a general election was around the corner. Now that he is no longer with us, we see the wisdom in the style of leadership which he adopted.

Mrs Lynch regretted that there had been a loss of outstanding young men throughout the Caribbean. Brilliant men from Grenada, Dominica and many other islands were in the outside world making remarkable contributions but their own lands were without their services. 'Let us thank God,' concluded the Senator, 'that Tom Adams loved his country enough to resist the beckoning of the outside world and to return here to work and die for this country.'[9]

David Seale recalled that, although Tom Adams was not widely regarded as a racing fan, he knew his racing as well as many and better than most. He could tell the Senator, whose knowledge of racing matters is encyclopedic, that, when Larkspur won the Derby in 1962, seven horses fell on Tottenham Corner. He could also tell him that Psidium won it at 66:1.

There were other conversations that enthralled the Senator. When he admired the grandfather clock at Ilaro Court, Tom could tell him where he could get a similar clock, the price of it and complete information on its workings. During a visit to Spain, they visited a famous cemetery and Tom could tell him the history of every tomb. To the Senator, who ran a supermarket business, among other things, it was a matter of great surprise that he knew the price of every article. He knew the best vintage year of wine, the best types of champagne and the price of each type.[10]

Senator John Jordan said that as a schoolboy he used to visit the public gallery of the House of Assembly and was impressed by Adams' depth of thought, his eloquence and his concern for the people. He considered that his life and work would be an inspiration to the young people of Barbados. He agreed with Senator Seale that his contribution might one day be equalled but never surpassed.[11]

Senator Herbie Yearwood believed that he was one of the persons in the Senate who enjoyed a long association with the late Prime Minister. He was at school with him in Barbados and their relationship developed more in the United Kingdom as they lived at different times in the same flat. Tom was a very senior member in the Earls Court branch of the British Labour Party and he himself became Vice-Chairman. He expressed satisfaction over the respect in which Tom was held and noted the readiness with which so many leaders from all over the world accepted the invitation to attend his funeral.[12]

Senator L.A. Ward could not claim to know the late Prime Minister very well but he associated himself with the sentiments that had been expressed about his contribution to Barbados and the Caribbean. Tom Adams always listened sympathetically to those who brought the problems of the sugar industry to his notice and they were grateful for the full support he gave the industry.[13]

David Simmons, a Government Member, said that he knew Adams from October 1960 when he had just entered London University and Tom was working with the BBC at Bush House in Aldwych. He was unpopular with some for two reasons. First, because he was Sir Grantley's son; and secondly because they could not cope with his massive intellect. Yet there were others who realised that he was readying himself for leadership. Simmons first realised this from a remark made at the Student Centre by Radcliff Hewitt. The latter saw Tom watching television and reading something at the same time. 'He is going to be a Prime Minister of Barbados: the fellow is just too bright,' said Hewitt at a time when Tom was going through a period of unpopularity owing to the impending dissolution of the WI Federation of which his father was Prime Minister.

7

Hutson Linton, a Government Member, reported to the Senate an interesting exchange with Tom Adams. After his first defeat in St Philip South, Tom asked him to serve in the Upper Chamber for a second term. Later he was invited to the PM's office:

Question: Hutson, have you been attending the Senate regularly?

Answer: As regularly as I have time to permit, Mr Prime Minister.

Question: Have you been getting there punctually?

Answer: As punctually as my business would allow me to.

Question: Having attended as regularly as your business would permit and attended as punctually as your business would permit, have you been making the contributions that you were making in your first term in the Senate?

Answer: As much as my business would allow me.

Tom then declared that he had received complaints to the contrary and expressed the hope that reports in the future would be more favourable.

Later the exchange took on a different character and Linton was again spoken to by the PM.

PM: Hutson, I know your attendance at Senate has improved.

Answer: So it has, Mr PM.

PM: You are even getting there early.

Answer: Yes, Mr PM.

PM: I notice you have made one or two contributions since I spoke to you.

Answer: Yes, Mr PM.

PM: You see what a little talking does to you now?

Answer: Right, Mr PM.

These exchanges provoked considerable amusement in the Senate. Linton explained, however, that he recounted them in order to show how Tom Adams treated the lowliest of his colleagues, showing no preference for one member of the Party over another.[14]

Miss June Clarke, a Government Senator, expressed concern over the fact that people who considered themselves responsible citizens had 'studiously and deliberately' sought for a long time to influence the innocent and the unsuspecting to believe that Tom Adams was a demon, if not 'the personification of Satan'. Yet she was consoled by what was now being said of him. 'As I listen to the glowing tributes paid to him from near and far, we cannot help being proud of this son of the soil who has so distinguished himself as a world class statesman.'[15]

Mrs Gwen Reader, an Independent Member, felt there was very little left to be said after all the speeches that had been made in the Senate. She contented herself by quoting the words of Shakespeare: 'He was my friend, faithful and just to me'; 'My heart is in the coffin there with Caesar,/And I must pause till it come back to me.'[16]

Mrs Milroy Reece, a Government Member, said she had not yet recovered from the passing of Tom Adams and felt unable to express her feelings without strain. But she mentioned some of the tributes that came over the radio. One person had said: 'I wish God could give me his brain.' Another said it should be donated to the Museum. 'People have said, with due respect to the Almighty, that they wished it had been them instead. People have said, 'I wanted to hate him, but I had to love him.' The comments that you hear from the ordinary folk on the road make me feel good about his passing.'[17]

The Deputy President, John Wickham, who was acting as President of the Senate, in the absence of Sir Arnott Cato, who was acting as Governor-General, brought the proceedings to an end with a short speech. He confessed that his own contact with Tom Adams was minimal. Though meeting him on rare occasions, it was still enough for him to have gained some sense of the quality of the man and to have been impressed by the range of his curiosity and his courageous appetite for knowledge. To Wickham he seemed to need desperately to know everything that there was to know and no aspect of human behaviour was too obscure to command his attention.

——————— 8 ———————

The moving tributes in the House and the Senate must have been a source of consolation to all of Tom's friends and relatives but especially to his mother, his wife and his two sons.

Genevieve, in spite of her grievous loss, was resolved to get on with her life and make it on her own. She obtained a job with an agency in Mackison Avenue, Manhattan, as from 16 November 1985, where she did its public relations for the Barbados Board of Tourism. After the general election of May 1986, the new Government took away its public relations account from the agency which employed her. She believed that, if she had remained in her original post, she might have lost her job. Fortunately, owing to her efficiency, she had been promoted within the company and set to work on investor relations. She was pleased with her promotion for two reasons. First, because it was a personal achievement and secondly, because it placed her beyond any victimisation that may have been intended.[18]

Thus Genevieve continued to make her way in a hard competitive world. She was sustained by the memory of her husband and the love and support of her sons. Without that love and support, she confessed, she could not have survived.[19]

The courage of the mother was equalled by that of her sons. Within a month of Tom's death, Douglas obtained an honours degree in history and two years

[margin annotation: Madison]

and three months later acquired an honours degree in law. Rawdon lost no time in pursuing a highly successful career in the University of South Carolina. There seems little doubt that Tom's two sons are determined to maintain the brilliance of the Adams tradition.

In the meantime Grace Adams continues to live at Tyrol Cot, alone, yet supported by the love of her many friends and admirers. In the slightly gloomy atmosphere of her home, memories of her husband and her son must have come crowding in upon her. Yet the night that covered her did not seem to be black as the pit from pole to pole. She did not wince nor cry aloud under the bludgeonings of chance nor in the fell clutch of circumstance.

Perhaps her spirit was sustained by her dreams during the long hours of darkness. Then she would relive the successes achieved, the failures overcome and happiness shared with her husband and her son. She would see them moving around the familiar places of Tyrol Cot. She would hear them talking and arguing endlessly about politics and every other subject in the world. They would wander in the richly-endowed library, seeking to quench their insatiable thirst for knowledge. They would go out into the gardens to see what beauty could be restored by the magic of their green thumbs.

With the dawn, her dreams of the night would fade, yet they seemed to remain with her as a waking reality. For death had no dominion over the two most important men in her life and she was sustained by the memory of their presence in the spacious house and grounds of Tyrol Cot.

What else could account for her calm dignity and inner strength during her most recent tragedy? Those who flocked to her side to console her soon found that it was Grace who consoled them. Broken with grief over the death of Tom Adams, they were gently urged by the Grand Old Lady not to regard his passing as a loss but to think of his life as a blessing. She would tell them that she was lucky to have had him for 53 years.[20]

No one has contributed more to Barbados than the gracious chatelaine of Tyrol Cot. She has given her husband, her son and herself to the island and its people. For this reason I have ventured to dedicate this book to her as a slender token of the esteem and affection in which she is universally held.

Notes

1. Hansard, Senate Debates (Official Report) 18 March 1985, pp. 665–6.
2. Ibid., p.667.
3. Hansard, Senate Debates, 28 March 1985, pp. 667–8.
4. Ibid., pp. 668–9.
5. Hansard, Senate Debates, 18 March 1985, pp. 669–70.
6. Ibid., p. 671.
7. Ibid., pp. 673–4.
8. Ibid., pp. 671–3.
9. Ibid., pp. 676–9.
10. Ibid., p. 679.
11. Ibid., pp. 679–80.
12. Ibid., pp. 680–81.
13. Ibid., p. 681.
14. Ibid., pp. 685–7.
15. Ibid., pp. 687–8.
16. Ibid., p. 682.
17. Ibid., pp. 688–9.
18. Letter from Genevieve Adams to the author, 3 Nov. 1986.
19. Ibid.
20. Related to the author by Sir Carlisle and Lady Burton, 12 Dec. 1986.

Chronology

1931   24 September. Born in Barbados.

1950   Winner of Barbados Scholarship.

1951−4   Magdalen College, Oxford. Politics, Philosophy and Economics. Joined Oxford branch of the British Labour Party.

1954−62   Member of WI Students Union, Earls Court, London. First as Secretary, later as Vice-President.

1956   Senior member of Earls Court Branch of British Labour Party.

1957−62   Worked with the BBC where he met Genevieve, daughter of Philip Turner, Chairman of Civil Service Legal Society.

1958   Establishment of WI Federation, with his father as Prime Minister.
Enrolled as student at Gray's Inn.

1962   Obtained Class ii in law finals.
Marriage to Genevieve.
May. Dissolution of WI Federation.

1963   Return to Barbados.

1965   Secretary of Barbados Labour Party.

1966   June. Constitutional Conference in London.
3 November. Won a seat in the Barbados House of Assembly.
30 November. Barbados became independent state with Errol Barrow as first Prime Minister.

1971   Leader of the Opposition

1974   Debate on Constitutional Amendments

1976   Prime Minister of Barbados

1977   April. Commonwealth Heads of Government Meeting in London.
Sept. Commonwealth Finance Ministers Meeting in Barbados.
Oct. World Bank Meeting in Washington.

1978 Sept. World Bank Meeting in Washington.
1979 July. Commonwealth Heads of Government Meeting in Zambia.
      Oct. World Bank Meeting in Yugoslavia.
      Dec. Units of Barbados Defence Force sent to foil attempted coup in St Vincent.
1980 World Bank Meeting in Washington.
1981 June. Re-elected Prime Minister of Barbados.
      Oct. Commonwealth Heads of Government Meeting in Australia.
1982 Annual CARICOM Heads of Government Meeting revived, in Jamaica, after lapse of nine years.
1983 May. CARICOM Heads Meeting in St Lucia.
      July. CARICOM Heads Meeting in Trinidad.
      Oct. Rescue Mission to Grenada.
      Nov. Commonwealth Heads of Government Meeting in Delhi.
1984 July. CARICOM Heads of Government Meeting in Nassau.
      Sept. Commonwealth Finance Ministers Meeting in Toronto.
      Oct. World Bank annual meeting in Washington.
1985 Feb. Visited Japan to negotiate loan.
      Canada-West Indies meeting in Jamaica.
1985 11 March. Died in Barbados.

Index

Acton Club, 9
Adams, Douglas (son), 25, 29, 139, 190−91
Adams, Genevieve (wife), née Turner:
engagement, 22; first meeting, 18−19; life, with Tom, 28−9; marriage, 22, 23, 29−30; and music, 29; as widow, 190
Adams, Lady Grace (mother), née Thorne:
early life, 2; marriage of, 1, 2, 183−4; strength of, 191−2; as teacher, 1, 4, 183
Adams, Sir Grantley (father):
contribution by, 159; marriage of, 1, 2; outspokenness of, 3−5; political career, 34−5, 36−7, 44−5, 125; suspension of, 47; Tom's quarrels with, 26−7; Tom's relationship with, 31
Adams, Rawdon (son), 25, 29, 191
Adams, Tom:
achievements, 102−3; birth of, 1, 184; cardiac failure, 141; as chairman of BLP, 51; questioning of, 55−6; character, 16, 17, 158−60; childhood', 2−10; and 'the common touch', 8; as communicator, 90−91, 152; contribution, 159−60; death of, 143, 161−2; election to Assembly, 38−9; as a father, 29; humanity of, 146−7; ill-health, 2, 6−7, 139; last days, 141−4; as Minister of Finance, 149−50; oratory in House, 76, 166, 168, 172; organisational flair, 37, 39−40, 51, 81; physical appearance, 30; as Prime Minister, 83−144; as QC, 147; socialist ideals, 148−9;
statemanship, 156; tributes to, 163−90
Alleyne, Sydney Burnett:
and banking, 75; invasion threat from, 83, 85
Arthur, Owen:
tribute to Tom, 173−4

Banking, 75
Alleyne Mercantile Bank, 75
Barbadian society:
changes in, 34
Barbados:
return to, from London, 24, 25
Barbados Development Bank, 90
Barbados National Party, 39
Barbados Progressive League, 34, 88
Barbados Scholarship, 10
to Oxford, 13
Barbados Workers Union, 34, 88
Barrow, Errol, 36, 40, 118
and constitution Bill, 57−64; contribution of, 159−60; death of, 159; and DLP, 78−80; as party leader, 79−80; popularity in Barbados, 47, 81; as Prime Minister, 44, 45, 52; as QC, 147; tribute to Tom, 175−6
Barrow, Nigel, Leader of Senate:
tribute to Tom, 177−8
BBC, British Broadcasting Corporation: Genevieve at, 18, 19; Tom at, 18, 20, 22, 91, 152
Bishop, Maurice: of Grenada, 111−15
Blackman, Dr Don, 84
and social development, 93−4
BLP, Barbados Labour Party, 27−8, 34, 38, 80−81, 175, 176; achievements, 102−3; co-operation with Tom, 39−40; election defeats, 27−8, 49; election victories, 83; organisational need in, 37, 51, 98−9; 1978 Party Conference address, 99−105; rebuilding, 30, 171; Tom as Chairman, 51; questioning of, 55−6
Bradshaw, Robert:
Premier, St Kitts-Nevis, 107−8
Bridge: interest in, 21−2
Bridgetown, City of:
1976 by-election, 82−3, 151
British Labour Party:
association with, 20, 22
Budget speeches:
1972: 52; 1976:73−6; 1981: 96

Bushe Experiment, 34, 124, 125

Caribbean Labour Congress, 34
Caribbean Service:
   producer for, 19
Caribbean Trade, Investment and
   Development conference, 1981:
   154—5
CARICOM, 135—6, 153, 160, 162
   5th Conference of, 135—6, 154
CARIFTA, 160
Cato, Milton:
   Premier of St Vincent, 109
CBI, Caribbean Basin Initiative,
   156
Cheltenham, Dr R. L.:
   tribute to Tom, 168—9
Clarke, Mrs June, Senator:
   tribute to Tom, 189
Commerce:
   Government participation in,
   104—5
Communism:
   anti-feeling to, 100
Constitution of Barbados:
   amendment Bill, 1974: 56—64;
   Barrow's speech, 56—64; Tom's
   speech, 66—73; views on, 124,
   125, 126—7; Cox Commission for
   the Protection of the -, 128—31
Constitutional Conference, 1966:
   report of, 69
Cooking: as hobby, 29
Co-operative societies, 133
Cox, Sir Mencea, 31, 35—6, 129, 184
Cox Commission, 129—31
Craig, Lionel:
   support of, 55; suspension of, 47
Credit Unions, 133
Cricket: as hobby, 8, 9, 22
Cuba:
   revolutionary movement from,
   110—11
Cubana air disaster, 83—4, 185
Cummins, Dr H. G.:
   Barbados Premier, 35—6, 148

Development:
   national, 101—2; at
   Speightstown, 137—8; in north,
   138
Dingle Foot's chambers:
   work at, 23
DLP, Democratic Labour Party, 28,
   36, 88, 103, 175, 176; and Barrow,
   78—80

Economic Survey, Barbados, 54

Economy, of Barbados:
   difficulties of, 52—4, 64, 66,
   85—7, 89—90; diversification, 73;
   and industrialisation, 157;
   recovery, 91, 95—6, 163; and
   world recession, 133—4; and
   1972 budget, 52
Education:
   increased facilities for, 91—3

Finance, Minister of, 149—50
Financial:
   assistance, need for, 30—31;
   Barbados as offshore centre, 150,
   157; crisis in Barbados, 87
Forde, Henry, 42, 91, 147
   Attorney-General, 111, 131; and
   Constitution Bill, 57—63, 131;
   early friendship, 23; and
   education development, 91—2;
   tribute to Tom, 170—71
Funeral, state:
   of Tom, 161—2

Gaitskell, Hugh:
   unofficial personal assistant, 15
General election, 1976: 83
Gray's Inn:
   student of, 20
Great Combination, The, 95, 96,
   127
Greaves, Evelyn:
   tribute to Tom, 179
Grenada:
   coup in, 111; New Jewel
   Movement in, 112; rescue
   mission, 114—22; revolution in,
   111—22, 185; Barbados role
   against, 114—22
Grenadines, 109, 110
Griffith, Clyde:
   tribute to Tom, 182—3
Gross National Product, 74
Gross Domestic Product:
   increase in, 134

Harrison College:
   schooling at, 6—7; training, 20
Hawkins Memorial Prize, 10
Haynes, Dr R. C.:
   tribute to Tom, 169—70
Health:
   and cardiac trouble, 139, 141,
   143; in childhood, 2, 6—7; at
   Oxford, 13
Hobbies, 15, 42, 43, 167, 168
Holder, Fabian, Barbados scholar,
   14

Holder, Gladstone:
  view of Tom, 125–7
Home help programme, 94
House of Assembly, Barbados:
  childhood visits by Tom, 8–9;
  Grantley Adams speeches in, 3,
  45; Tom's election to, 38–9;
  Tom's speeches in, 43
Housing development, 90

Ilaro Court:
  official residence, 142, 143
Independence of Barbados:
  11th anniversary, 89–90
Infrastructure:
  importance of, 157
International Confederation of
  Free Trade Unions:
  and Sir Grantley Adams, 35, 108;
  and Robert Bradshaw, 108

Jemmott, Clarence:
  tribute to Tom, 183
Jones, Canon Ivor:
  tribute to Tom, 180
Jordan, John, Senator:
  tribute to Tom, 186

Law:
  career, in Barbados, 42, 43;
  discrimination against, 147;
  training in, 19
Leadership, of Tom, 170, 178, 185,
  187
Linton, Hudson:
  tribute to Tom, 187–8
London:
  life in, 81–24
Lynch, Mrs Enid:
  as educator, 92–3; tribute to
  Tom, 183–6

Magdalen College, Oxford:
  building, 12; spirit of, 11–12;
  Tom at, 11
Manufacturing industry:
  decline, 73; growth, 86, 95; and
  infrastructure, 157
Mapp, Sir Ronald, 31, 38, 39, 41,
  148
Marriage:
  to Genevieve Turner, 23
Marshall Plan, 155–6
Marxism:
  in Grenada, 112; ideological
  assault by, 99–100
McClean, Wendall:
  tribute to Tom, 181

Media:
  1971–6 blackout complaint by
  BLP, 76
Miller, Billie, 82
  tribute to Tom, 171–2
Moscow: visit to, 19, 179
Multilateral Clearing Facility, 165
  collapse of, 169

Nation, the (newspaper):
  tribute to Tom in, 163–4
National Union of Public Workers,
  53

OECS, Organisation of Eastern
  Caribbean States:
  and Grenada, 115, 116
Organisation in politics:
  Tom's flair for, 37, 39–40, 51, 81
Oxford Labour Party:
  member of, 14, 24
Oxford University:
  degree at, 14–15; interests at,
  14–15; Tom at, 10, 11–17

Payne, Clement:
  trade unionist, 33, 87
Poker:
  addiction to, 22, 142
Politics:
  as orator, 152; preparation for,
  23–4; realities of, 36–7;
  strategies in, 51; Tom's
  enjoyment of, 175
Protectionism:
  of trade, 135–6
Public Service:
  and political discrimination,
  103–4, 126, 127

Racing: as hobby, 186
Reader, Mrs Gwen, Independent
  Member:
  tribute to Tom, 189
Reece, Mrs Milroy, Government
  Member:
  tribute to Tom, 189
Relaxation:
  gift for, 15
Revolt, of 1937:
  commemoration of, 87–9
Road-building, 149–50

St John, Bernard, 38, 39–40, 147; as
  chairman of BLP, 48–9, 51, 81;
  as Deputy Prime Minister, 95,
  143; tribute to Tom, 164–5

St Lucia:
  and Cuban movements, 111
St Michael's Girls' School, 1, 4, 5,
  183
St Peter:
  1984 by-election, 139
St Philip North:
  1976 by-election, 81
St Thomas constituency, 142, 169
  Tom's election, 38, 43
St Vincent:
  attempted coup, 109–10
Sandiford, Erskine:
  tribute to Tom, 172–3
Schlesinger, Arthur, Jr.:
  and Grenada issue, 120–21
Scientific socialism, 100–101
Seale, David, Senator:
  tribute to Tom, 186
Secondary Teachers Union, 53, 181
Senators:
  tributes to Tom by, 186–7
Share ownership:
  in businesses, 133
Simmons, David, Government
  Member, 81
  tribute to Tom, 187
Social democracy, 132–3
Social development, 93–4
Socialist International :
  Barbadian membership, 101
Spalding, Stuart, philatelist, 15–17
  holidays with, 16
Speightstown development, 137–8
Springer, H. W. (Sir Hugh),
  Governor-General, 34, 184
Stamp-collecting: as hobby, 15,
  16
Stoll, George, 21
  as best man, 23
Sugar production, 73, 79, 95;
  dispute in, 79; fluctuation of, 54
'Sunset', Enterprise Road:
  Tom's home in Barbados, 28, 30
Supreme Court of Judicature Bill,
  43–44

Taitt, Branford:
  tribute to Tom, 165–7
Taxation, 149
  Tom as 'tax collector', 149

Tenantry Freehold Purchase Act,
  132
Tourism:
  benefits from, 90; decline in, 73,
  75; growth, 86, 95
Trade unionism:
  in Barbados, 33
Travels:
  in Europe, 18; to Moscow, 19;
  up the Nile, 122; to USA, 55
Trotman, O'Brian:
  tribute to Tom, 180–81
Tull, Louis:
  Attorney-General, 115; tribute to
  Tom, 167–9; views on Tom, 117,
  150
Tyrol Cot, family home, 3, 5, 191
  arson attempt, 33; building, 25;
  library at, 184; problems at,
  25–8; Tom's visits to, 36–7;
  visitors to, 26, 184

Unemployment:
  rate, 75, 95, 134; work for, 90
Union Island, St Vincent:
  revolt on, 109–10
Ursuline Convent:
  Tom's early school, 4
United States:
  Barbadian relations with, 156–7;
  and Grenada revolution, 116–19

Walcott:
  'Dick', 42; Edward Keith,
  Attorney-General, 9, 42, 124–5;
  Frank, 34, 40, 70, 184
Ward, Justice Deighton, 59–61
Ward, L. A., Senator:
  tribute to Tom, 187
West Indian Service:
  of BBC, producer at, 22
West Indian Student Centre, 24;
  Vice-President of, 20–21
West Indies Federation, 28, 164;
  dissolution of, 159; and Sir
  Grantley Adams, PM, 35
Wickham, John, Deputy President:
  tribute to Tom, 189–90

Yearwood, Herbie, Senator:
  tribute to Tom, 186–7